HOW MUCH MORE?

*Discovering the Depths
of the Father's Love*

GOLFRAN A. RIVERA

WESTBOW
PRESS®
A DIVISION OF THOMAS NELSON
& ZONDERVAN

WestBow Press books may be ordered through booksellers or by contacting:

WestBow Press
A Division of Thomas Nelson & Zondervan
1663 Liberty Drive
Bloomington, IN 47403
www.westbowpress.com
844-714-3454

ISBN: 978-1-6642-4972-1 (sc)
ISBN: 978-1-6642-4973-8 (hc)
ISBN: 978-1-6642-4971-4 (e)

Library of Congress Control Number: 2021923137

Print information available on the last page.

WestBow Press rev. date: 11/23/2021

CONTENTS

To the church in the West. Grace and peace to you
from God, our Father, and the Lord Jesus Christ.

PREFACE

Before I formed you in the womb, I knew you.
—Jeremiah 1:5 (ESV)

I'll never forget that moment of watching my oldest son on that ultrasound screen, dancing around in his mother's womb. The euphoria! The utter joy as I celebrated with my wife the coming of our firstborn child. At the time, I didn't know he was a boy. All I knew was that I had loved him before he was formed in the womb.

My wife and I married at a young age. I was nineteen and she was eighteen years old. We decided to wait several years before conceiving simply because we wanted to invest time into our marriage. We had dated for a total of four months before getting married. Trust me: you are *not* the only ones who wondered if it was a shotgun wedding. But even though we did not attempt to conceive a little one for at least five years, we had been planning a life as a family since before we were married. We made so many decisions based on the hopeful idea that we would one day bring into this world little children to bless and love.

As a couple, we would go over different scenarios and discuss what we would do and why. How would we work out the sleep schedule with a newborn? What would we do if one day they said they wanted to quit school? What happens if one of us corrects the child in a way the other one doesn't like? We agreed that whatever we would eventually do, we knew that the plans we had for them would be to prosper them and not to harm them, plans to give them a hope and a future.

We eventually moved to beautiful North Carolina. Before actually making the move, we searched online for the "perfect home" that would house our future family. We wanted a space for them to play and grow. We didn't want too much opportunity for them to isolate themselves in their rooms, so we looked for a big yard and spacious family living areas. We wanted a large kitchen to share memories in. And we looked for a dining room that was far away from the television so we could break bread as a family and commune together at the dinner table. Far before the day our first child was even conceived, we had gone to prepare a place where we would take them to be with us that they also may be where we were.

When I discovered that my firstborn child would be a boy, my heart swelled with emotion. How could it be? *How could it be that God would willingly surrender His only Son to die for my sins?* My child wasn't even born yet, and already the thought of giving him up to a world that would hate him and curse his name devastated me. I wanted to shield him and teach him to defend himself. I couldn't imagine raising him to be a sacrifice for the crimes of others!

As we walked out of the ultrasound appointment, I wept. I had only just started to really understand the depth of the Father's love for me.

Eventually, we had a newborn on our hands. It was wonderful, but man, was it exhausting! At my worst, I had to step away from the baby. I was so exhausted, and he was just so inconsolable at times. The frustration would get the better of me and I would need to put the baby down and walk away. But then in the morning, with my eyes burning from lack of sleep, I would rush to grab him from his crib, put him on my side of the bed, and love on him, kiss him, and squeeze him. He would usually spit up after being breastfed. Always on my side of the bed. But I just wanted to love on him and clean him, and I looked forward to a new day with him. Man ... the Father's love.

When I was at my best during those long nights, getting up to rock the baby and give my wife a chance to rest, I would read God's Word to him. I would pray over him and ask God for favor over his life. I would ask God for wisdom and for the ability to be a good father for him. And then on one occasion, as I was reading through the gospel of Matthew, holding this little person in my arms, I read the words I had read so many times before. "If you then, who are evil, know how to give good gifts to your children, how much more does your Father in heaven give good gifts to those who ask Him?"[1] Wow! God was inviting me to really begin to understand the depth of the Father's love.

I had been told more times than I can count that children have a way of changing you. Being young and naive, I refused to believe that it could be true. I considered myself a man of principles. These principles would not yield to a newborn. What I could have never imagined is the way God has been using my children to transform the way I understand His love for me as His son. And for some time now, I have felt the burden on my heart to share this reality with you.

I want to share this in two separate parts. First, I want to help us understand ourselves. As His children, what is it on our end that prevents us from embracing the fullness of His love? It is both our past wounds and our own sinful nature. I want to talk frankly with you about this and hopefully help us wrestle with these major obstacles that often find themselves deeply rooted in our hearts.

Secondly, and perhaps most importantly, I want to share with you His character. I want us to look deeply into the person of God the Father. Having looked in the mirror and seen a reflection of ourselves, I want us to look higher to the One who calls us His. I want us to discover just how deep the Father's love goes for us.

This book has been birthed from a desire to express to you the profound reality of being a child of God. To capture the journey of walking in fellowship with Father God. To invite you into a level of intimacy with your loving Father that transcends philosophies, denominations, liturgy, or anything else that replaces the reality of being an adopted son or daughter of God. My hope is that you will walk away from this book encouraged and inspired to see yourself the way He sees you, as His very own child. I hope you will believe Christ when He said that it is the Father's good pleasure to give us the kingdom. I hope that when you have finished reading, you will understand that if you and I, though we are evil, know how to give good gifts to our children, how much more will our Father in heaven give the Holy Spirit to those who ask?

PART 1

OUR OWN HEARTS

CHAPTER 1

WOUNDS FROM OUR FATHERS

Fathers, do not embitter your children,
or they will be discouraged.
—Colossians 3:21 (NIV)

I'm not sure the kind of impact a father has on a child can be overstated. Fathers are meant to be leaders in the household. For a man, the father figure becomes the one to confirm his manhood and to show him what it means to be a man. For a woman, the father is the first to show her how to be revered and honored by men. When the father is absent, or unloving or abusive, he can leave emotional wounds that hinder his children's relationships with others. These wounds can ultimately embitter children and discourage them from experiencing the pure love of their Father in heaven.

THE FATHER WOUND

Now I love my dad very much. I am blessed to call him Dad. With that being said, he was far from perfect. He was very absent during my childhood. He was often gone drinking with his brothers, fixing cars with his brothers, riding dirt bikes with his brothers, or playing soccer with his brothers. There were too many instances to count when he would leave me to play by myself, while I hoped we were to be bonding as father and son. But he would go off and be with his brothers.

There is one particular memory I'm not sure I'll ever forget. My dad has always been a soccer fanatic. He watched every soccer league available on TV, and he never missed a single World Cup game. He was an avid forward on his brother's soccer team. They regularly won games and championships at their local soccer leagues. I was not very good at soccer.

He once tried to put me, as a goalie, into a match that was already underway, and I embarrassed us by not really knowing how to put the ball into play. He definitely wanted me to follow in his footsteps, but he just never seemed to have the time to teach me. You can imagine how excited I was when he said he would be available to practice with me in our driveway. He had no appointments with any of his brothers or his friends. So this was going to be my chance. We started to kick the ball around in the driveway.

Only a few minutes had gone by when my uncle showed up. He wanted to talk to my dad about a car they had been working on that was parked farther down the driveway. My dad paused our game and said, "Just for a second." Then he went to look at the car. The seconds turned into minutes, and those minutes eventually caused me to become heartbroken. I kicked the ball by myself against the wall of the house. I felt silly waiting out there for a father who would never come, so I decided to give up and go inside.

I grew up wondering why it seemed like I just wasn't worth my father's time. I was embarrassed that I wasn't good enough at the things he was interested in. Aside from not getting enough father-son time with my dad, I rarely, if ever, received praise. Instead, despite my best efforts, it was more common for him to criticize me and highlight what it was I failed to do rather than compliment me for what it was I may have accomplished.

Whether it was cleaning the house, mowing the lawn, building something, succeeding in school, or performing in speech and debate, there was rarely any confirmation that what I was doing mattered to him. What I knew for certain was that I hadn't cleaned the floors well enough, that I didn't make the lines on the lawn straight enough, that I didn't build that doghouse sturdy enough, that I didn't study enough, and that speech and debate wasn't interesting enough. I was left wounded by my father, convinced I wasn't enough.

The reality is that my experience isn't unique, and it isn't even the worst of experiences. Millions of people endure the painful abuse of violent fathers. Millions of children around the world are growing up without their fathers. They were either abandoned or lost their dads to tragic circumstances. These experiences with our fathers leave their mark. They leave what some psychologists call "the father wound." This wound can often be what stands between us and embracing the profound love of God the Father.

TROUBLE WITH AUTHORITY

The truth is that our fathers aren't the only people in our lives who are in a position to harm us. Really, anyone who has ever had some kind of authority in our lives has the power to tear us down or build us up. When these people use their authority to hurt us, the emotional and sometimes physical scars can become barriers in our hearts and minds, which keep us at a distance from the Father's love.

Teachers who make students feel unintelligent, friends who make their friends feel insignificant, and mothers who criticize their children, for example. These people in our lives have access to our hearts. And when they don't steward that access with love and respect, they can cause serious damage. That fact is tragic in and of itself, but the greater tragedy is that the damage done by others stays with us, and we ultimately project the resulting insecurities onto our Father in heaven.

Unfortunately, to make matters worse, it seems that one of the most common wounds we endure is from "religious" people. We view these people as having the authority to represent the person of God. So when they hurt us, disappoint us, or commit heinous crimes, supposedly in His name, we can't help but conclude that God is a violent, judgmental, malicious being.

Some of us have been cast out by churchgoers, criticized by judgmental people, and made to feel that God's love does not extend to us. For me, the fact that my dad claimed to be a believer yet treated me the way that he did led me to conclude that God was unloving and cold. I didn't want anything to do with Him.

People are flawed, but they have access to our hearts. When they mishandle that privilege, they cause wounds that cut deep. And when that happens, it is only natural that we project our wounds onto our Father in heaven.

PROJECTING OUR WOUNDS

We may not always be aware of it, but a lot of the emotional baggage we accumulate throughout our lives is often brought into our most intimate relationships. While we may be able to keep those burdens hidden from strangers or acquaintances, intimacy with someone has a way of drawing that pain out of us. For that reason, when we've been hurt, we have a way of keeping our distance from people. It's not always obvious to us or to others, but we keep our deepest hurts hidden away and remain cautious in how much of ourselves we're willing to really share. Our relationship with the Father is no exception.

Think about your opinion of the Father's heart toward you. Does He consider you a sinner or a saint washed by the blood of His Son? Does He look at you as someone who is undeserving of love, or does He love you so much that He gave His only Son for you? What does He require from you: undying servitude or unconditional love? The answers to these questions stem from the depth of our hearts. Where there is emotional baggage, there is less room for a clear picture of God's love toward us. We will keep a distance from Him and inadvertently choose to believe that He holds things against us, or that we have to work to earn His favor, or any number of untrue, unbiblical beliefs about Him.

Our deepest wounds have a way of clinging on to us. They can be so deep-rooted that we may not even realize how much they fog our way of thinking. I did not realize that when I came into a relationship with God, what stood out to me the most about Him was His perfect standards. But this should come as no surprise since I grew up with a dad who had to have things done a very particular way. I also struggled with the insecurity that if I did do something wrong, or if I didn't do something well enough, I would miss out on His favor and His blessings.

I was often paralyzed by the fear that I would do something to disappoint God. I connected my behavior to God's behavior, as if how He treated me depended completely on how I behaved. It was not until that night when I was carrying my *own* son and reading God's Word that I began to understand what it meant to be held in the Father's arms as His son. For the first time, the apostle John's words started to come alive in my heart. "See what kind of love the Father has given to [you], that [you] should be called [child] of God; and so [you] are."[1]

We all battle with this problem of projecting insecurities toward God our Father. Some of us do so consciously. But most of us don't even realize that part of the reason we remain distant from His love is because of low expectations created by our earthly fathers or mothers or anyone else in our lives who was a figure of authority. We can be scared to trust God with our future because we were never able to depend on our fathers to provide for us. We might not be convinced His grace is sufficient because people in our lives have held our past against us so often. But if we're going to embrace the fullness of His love and the power of His gospel, we must be willing to identify our past wounds and invite Him to heal us.

INCREASING OUR EXPECTATIONS

It's possible that by the time you read this book, your expectations of your Heavenly Father's love are low. Maybe you don't see it that way. Maybe you think it's reasonable to expect punishment for doing the wrong things or to be concerned about doing enough for the kingdom. By now it might seem natural to think of your relationship with God the Father in terms of church attendance, prayers prayed, or the amount of scripture you've memorized. And none of these activities are bad in and of themselves, but I believe that when we gauge the love of our Father in heaven by these things it is because our expectations have been lowered by the wounds that people have dealt us.

I know that the love I have for my children is not based on their performance. It is unearned and not sustained by their behavior. My love for them is a reflection of my heart, not theirs. In a much more perfect way, the Father's love for us stems from *His* heart, not our performance.

Now there remains one more important topic to discuss before we can dive deeper into that reality. But for now, I invite you to reflect on your past hurts and ask yourself how they may be standing in the way of your receiving the love of the Father in a much purer way.

CHAPTER 1 REFLECTIONS

1. What are some wounds that you still carry around in your heart? Think it over and write them down.

2. How are you projecting these wounds onto your Heavenly Father?

3. What will it take for you to accept the healing that Jesus Christ secured for you through His gospel?

Prayer Invitation

The Lord invites us to lay our burdens down at His feet. He says, "Come to me, all you who are weary and burdened, and I will give you rest."[2] He invites us to let go of the past hurts and to enter a new life in His presence. You can pray for God to help you relinquish the bitterness and to help you forgive those who have wounded you. Pray that you would see His love with such clarity that you would no longer know the sting of past hurts. In Jesus's name, amen.

CHAPTER 2

IF YOU THEN,
WHO ARE EVIL

But your iniquities have made a separation between
you and your God, and your sins have hidden His
face from you so that He does not hear.
—Isaiah 59:2 (ESV)

Many of you read the last chapter and felt that my experiences with
my father really resonated with you. I hope that if it did, it might
have provided some genuine insight into your relationship with
your own father and how it has affected your relationship with
your Father in heaven. But the truth is not everyone grows up with
a challenging relationship with their father. Not everyone has an
especially tough time relating to their parents. Some of us are raised
in very healthy relationships with our parents. Praise God for that!
Still, whether you were raised in a happy home or you found yourself
in constant conflict with your parents, something I know to be true
of all of us is that we wrestle with a misconstrued view of God.

This doesn't mean that you don't know God at all. What I mean
is that we have all at some point in our lives not grasped the depth
and width of the Father's love. At some point in time, we have given
way to our emotions and our own misconceptions about God, and it

has impacted the way we commune with Him. We have all allowed shame or guilt to keep us at a distance from His grace. There are times when we just don't feel comfortable coming to Him with our issues or with our mistakes. Many of us aren't always sure that our desires are worth His attention. In some form or fashion, we have all been guilty of missing the extent of the Father's love for us.

I know this because not only have I experienced it in my own life, and not only have I spoken to countless believers who too have felt this, but the Lord testifies about this in His Word. We have all at some point given way to something that prevented us from seeing God clearly. We have all sinned and fallen short of the glory of God.

MISSING THE MARK

There is a modern teaching among various congregations that says that the word *sin* "simply means to miss the mark." Now I'm not a Hebrew scholar so I am not in the position to confirm or deny this teaching. It may very well be that sin is the English translation of the Hebrew word for "missing the mark." But when we teach that sin is simply missing the mark, we do a great disservice to the listeners. The example that is often used is that of you aiming for a target and missing the mark. It seems rather inconsequential if I'm trying to shoot at something and I miss. Sure, I missed and I'm disappointed, but did I really lose anything? Not really. Teaching that it is simply missing the mark, in my humble opinion, *is* missing the mark—unless we use a more appropriate example.

Let us concede that sin does mean "to miss the mark." Well, rather than imagining that we are aiming at a target that we're shooting for, let us imagine we are standing at the edge of a cliff, facing a wide gap between our side of the cliff and another cliff across from us. We want to jump across the gap. Sinning is more like attempting to jump across this gap and missing the mark. You missed the other side and now you are plummeting to your death.

No big deal, right? No, it's a very big deal! And I'm not being overdramatic. Paul himself stated that "the wages of sin is death"![1] There are greater consequences to our sin than simply missing the mark.

In fact, going back through the history of creation, we see just how devastating sin really is. I don't have to remind you what the consequence of the first sin was. Along with the shame of disobedience, Adam and Eve were cast out from the presence of God. Their sin created enmity between both of them. It created pain for Eve and hard toil for Adam. The consequence of disobeying God and sinning against His word ultimately led to death and disease and destruction among humanity. It was no small thing then, and it is no small thing now.

For Cain, sin was responsible for the death of his brother! The Lord warned him that sin was crouching at the door, but Cain did not heed His warning. The world fell into chaos as people continued to fall deeper and deeper into sin and farther and farther away from God. Ultimately, God was so displeased with the wickedness of humankind that He "started over" with Noah.

We could go through the entire Bible and review all of human history, and we would find plenty of evidence that sin is no small thing. Perhaps the greatest proof of this was the moment Jesus hung on the cross. He did not hang on the cross because we simply missed the mark. He hung on the cross because "God made Him who had no sin to be sin for us, so that in Him we might become the righteousness of God."[2] It was because of our sins that Jesus needed to die. It was because we missed the other side of the cliff and fell into the gaping hole and plummeted to our deaths.

WHAT IS SIN?

We have come to an understanding that sin is no small thing. However, what exactly is sin? Better asked, what does God have to say about sin? In order for us to see how sin keeps us from the love of God, we should explore what God has to say about the matter.

Firstly, sin is the by-product of wrong desires. The apostle James states it clearly. "Each person is tempted when he is lured and enticed by his own desire. Then desire when it has conceived gives birth to sin, and sin when it is fully grown brings forth death."[3] In the Garden, Eve was enticed by the possibility of becoming like God. Though she had the whole earth and the very presence of God, she was tricked into thinking there could be more for her. Adam was deceived as well, and together they allowed temptation to give birth to their sinful disobedience.

It is no wonder Christ gives us the command to cut off our right hand or tear out our right eye if they cause us to sin. If we fill our hearts with wrong desires and allow temptation to linger around us, we are allowing the conception of sin within that will ultimately lead down the road of death. As the book of Proverbs wisely asks, "Can a man scoop a flame into his lap and not have his clothes catch on fire?"[4] Wherever there is wrong desire, there is an opportunity for sin to take hold of us and cause us to stumble.

More than the power to make us stumble, however, sin has the power to enslave. When Jesus was preaching to the Israelites, He declared that whoever held on to His truth would be set free. The people responded by saying that they had never been slaves of anyone. Essentially, they were implying they had no need for the freedom that Christ was offering them. But Christ's response was clear. "Truly, truly, I say to you, everyone who commits sin is the slave of sin."[5] Is this not what we are warned about all throughout the New Testament? Is that not what we have experienced in our own lives? That there is something at odds within us, battling to lead us down the wrong path? If we're being honest, we have all felt like Paul.

> I find this law at work: Although I want to do good,
> evil is right there with me. For in my inner being I

delight in God's law; but I see another law at work
in me, waging war against the law of my mind and
making me a prisoner of the law of sin at work
within me. What a wretched man I am! Who will
rescue me from this body that is subject to death?⁶

Being the product of wrong desires and having the power to
enslave us, sin is incredibly destructive. It has the power to destroy
not only our lives and the lives of those around us; it has the power
to seriously harm our relationship with our Father in heaven. This
is because "sin is lawlessness."⁷

We are children of a holy and righteous God. He and all His
ways are good. His Law is perfect. Sin stands in direct opposition of
who God is. It is not only missing the mark of your good intentions;
it is missing the mark of God's perfectly good Law. To allow desires
to give birth to sin in our lives, to allow ourselves to be enslaved by
sin, is to violate the Law of our Heavenly Father. It is to disobey His
commands and to undermine His purpose for creating us in the first
place. And in a relationship with our Father, how can we be at peace
with Him when we live in disobedience to Him? How can we say
we love Him when we don't obey Him?

When Adam and Eve sinned, they felt the shame of their
disobedience. They realized how exposed they were, and they hid
from the presence of God. Is that not what we are inclined to do
when we sin as well? As little children growing up, was it easy
to confess to our parents our disobedience? Especially when our
disobedience led to serious consequences? If we feared the wrath of
our parents, who by no means were able to set a perfect standard,
how much more will we be inclined to fear God when we know
that we have disobeyed His perfect Law? More than simply missing
the mark, sinful disobedience is the ultimate reason why we fail at
realizing the fullness of the Father's love for us.

NO ONE IS RIGHTEOUS

It may seem harsh to say, but the truth is that no one among is guiltless of sin. In fact, in God's words,

> There is no one righteous, not even one; there is no one who understands; there is no one who seeks God. All have turned away, they have together become worthless; there is no one who does good, not even one.[8]

We may want to consider ourselves or others generally good people, but that it is not what God has to say.

You've probably heard the opinion, maybe even held the opinion yourself, that people are generally good but that we are capable of great evil. However, as sweet as the sentiment behind this opinion might be, God's Word and human history testify that the opposite is true. People are generally evil, but they are capable of great good. Jesus Himself, in response to the young leader who called Him good teacher, said, "Why do you call Me good? No one is good except God alone."[9]

Are we willing to accept this fact? Are we willing to accept the words of Christ? We must accept them! Not only do we read it in His Word, but we see it in our lives. If we have fallen before God and prayed for His mercy, if we have cried out His name and begged for His forgiveness, then we must have accepted that what He has said about us and sin is true. In fact, "If we say we have no sin, we deceive ourselves, and the truth is not in us."[10] The truth is we do indeed have sin in us. And the truth is our sin separates us from the love of God.

While the thought of being evil may not be pleasant, it is still true. Yet it is also true that we are capable of much good. After all, we are made in the image of our good Father in heaven. While we may be sinners, we are also people who love and serve and help others. Not perfect by any means, but there is still some good in us, right? Imagine then, if we, being as evil as we are, are capable of such good, how much more is our Father in heaven? We are so evil that we often withhold forgiveness from others. We hold resentment toward others. We hurt others, and we hurt ourselves. Yet we would still sacrifice for the people we care about. We would still care for our own. So if we then who are evil know how to give good gifts to our children and to each other, how much more will our Father in heaven give the Holy Spirit—the Spirit of Comfort, the Spirit of Peace, the Spirit of *adoption* who cries out in our hearts, "Abba, Father"? How much more will our Father in heaven give good things to those who ask Him?

CHAPTER 2 REFLECTIONS

1. How has sin clouded your perception of God's love for you? Think of the times you've wanted to run and hide from Him or the times you've felt you didn't want to "burden" Him with your issues. What role did sin play in those situations?

2. What unconfessed sins hold you back from deeper intimacy with God? Why are you afraid to confess them? Are you afraid that the Father would not forgive you? Does holding onto this sin make you feel better or worse in the long run?

3. Do you believe that you are evil? What does God say? If you were evil, would that keep God from loving you?

Prayer Invitation

We are confronted with the harsh reality that our sin is evil in the sight of the Lord. Yet He came proclaiming the good news. He called us to "repent, for the Kingdom of Heaven is at hand."[11] We are invited to call upon the Lord for forgiveness of our sins. If there are sins that you have failed to confess or sins that you think might be hidden even from you, call out to your Father in heaven. "If we confess our sins, He is faithful and just to forgive us our sins and to cleanse us from all unrighteousness."[12] In Jesus's name. Amen.

PART 2

THE HEART OF THE FATHER

CHAPTER 3

FORGIVENESS AND HEALING

"He Himself bore our sins" in His body on the cross,
so that we might die to sins and live for righteousness;
"by His wounds you have been healed."
—1 Peter 2:24 (NIV)

Where do we go from here? Having looked in the mirror and seen in the reflection the face of someone dealing with wounds from the past or someone who is confronted with their own evil, what now? How do we go from projecting the insecurities of our pain and our guilt onto God to being fully loved by Him? The answer is Jesus Christ, the hope of glory.

You might have heard this before, but the term *gospel* actually means "good news." Jesus came preaching the good news of the kingdom of heaven. When asked by John's disciples if He was the One the people had been waiting for, Jesus replied (emphasis mine),

> Go back and report to John what you hear and see: The blind receive sight, the lame walk, those who have leprosy are cleansed, the deaf hear, the dead are raised, *and the good news* is proclaimed to the poor.[1]

What is good news if it is not in contrast to bad news?

The bad news we already know. The bad news is that many of us grew up being wounded by those we were supposed to be able to trust. We were raised (or even abandoned) by parents who didn't really know how to love us. We were torn down by those who should have been building us up. Because of that, we aren't really sure how to love others or even how to love ourselves. The bad news is that we have become slaves to sin. We have all, like lost sheep, gone astray. We have all been found guilty, by God, of violating His perfect Law. The bad news of all of this is that not only do we not see the love of the Father clearly, but we also stand condemned for our sins.

Jesus Christ, however, is the good news. He is the gospel that Paul preached. He is the One who was "pierced for our transgressions; He was crushed for our iniquities; upon Him was the chastisement that brought us peace, and with His wounds we are healed."[2]

The reality is that we cannot undo what has been done to us and what we ourselves are guilty of. We may be able to heal from the hurt of our past, and we may be able to try to live better lives in the hopes of reconciling our mistakes, but nothing we do today can undo what has been done yesterday. But God, who is much mightier than us, has been able to do what we in our own weakness could not. And this may not be news to you anymore. You may be so familiar with the gospel by now that you're ready to breeze through this chapter. But there is a reason I want us to abide in this message of Jesus for a second longer.

We've been talking about how the Father desires to reveal a deeper version of His love to us. And I believe that our appreciation for this revelation begins with a greater understanding of what exactly it means to be forgiven by Him. I have seen all too often brothers and sisters in Christ who are unable to fully embrace the freedom that comes with being a child of God through the gospel of Christ Jesus. Because of our past wounds or because of our sins, we have a tendency to add unnecessary, and often unbiblical, caveats to the gospel. So whether you have been walking with the Lord for some time or this book is your first genuine exposure to the gospel, let us dive a little deeper into what it means when Jesus says, "Your sins are forgiven" and "Your faith has made you whole."

FORGIVEN IN ADVANCE

If you're anything like me, you've either been hurt by someone or you've been guilty of hurting someone. In either case, when a wrong is done, if there is to be any kind of reconciliation, there needs to be forgiveness. Unfortunately, many of us struggle to forgive others. We all have our own reasons for it. I have found that the hardest people to forgive are people that I'm not actually intimate with.

But I've never had trouble forgiving my own children. When they were each born, they each took up all of my wife's attention. They both ended up soiling my side of the bed. They kept me from sleeping (my youngest child a lot more than my oldest). As they got older and more mobile, they started breaking things and losing things. They made traveling very difficult. Now that our oldest is two years old, he yells when he's upset, and he constantly battles for his independence. He explicitly disobeys us from time to time. He's thrown things at me and at his little brother. Sometimes he ignores us. On very rare occasions, he will throw a tantrum in an attempt to get his way. His younger brother really likes to cause a scene when he's unhappy. He's perfected his fake cry and is more than happy to share it with you when he doesn't get his way. He is more stubborn than big brother and often ignores what Mom and I say. Yet I forgive both for every wrong they have ever committed.

You may think, *Of course you forgive them. They're children.* But they're not just children. They're *my* children. They are *my* boys, in whom *I* am well pleased. They have not earned favor with me. They have not done anything to deserve my grace over their lives. They are my own, and no matter what, even when it hurts me, what I desire for them is peace and joy in their lives. I knew from before they were even conceived that they would sin against me. They would disobey my wife and me. They would be disrespectful, and if they were *anything* like me, they were going to do a lot of things behind our backs that I would probably be embarrassed to learn about. Yet I also knew from before they were conceived that I would love them deeply and that I would find a way for my grace to cover their lives.

The amazing truth is that while I am an imperfect father, our God in heaven is not. He, greater than I could, could see the many sins that we would commit against Him. He knew our stubbornness; He knew our hostility toward Him. He knew that our disobedience would go beyond throwing a tantrum. It would amount toward hate for one another. It would grow into genocide, rape, torture, and so many more tragic sins against those whom He made in His image. He knew this, about us, yet He loved us. In fact, "God decided in advance to adopt us into His own family by bringing us to Himself through Jesus Christ. This is what He wanted to do, and it gave Him great pleasure."[3]

This may be difficult to accept. Intellectually, a lot of us understand it. We could answer this question correctly on a test. Did God know you were going to sin? Yes. Did He forgive you anyway? Yes. Still, personally I have struggled to wrap my *heart* around this, and I have seen many brothers and sisters struggle with this as well. Our Father in heaven knew we would sin against Him, and He created us any way. And He loved us anyway. And He loved us freely, purely, and passionately. How can it be? He helped me see this once I held my own boy. Is it really that hard to believe that a perfect God would be capable of loving something that couldn't love Him back quite the same? Is it really hard to believe that the God who is love would be able to love His own people past their own faults? If I who is evil is capable of loving my son as such, how much more can my Father in heaven?

COMPLETE FORGIVENESS

But what about justice? What about righting the wrongs we have committed? How can we imagine that Almighty God, the Lord of lords, King of kings, and Righteous Judge of the whole universe would just overlook our sins? The answer, once again, is Jesus. More specifically, the answer is "God made Christ, who never sinned, to be the offering for our sin, so that we could be made right with God through Christ."[4]

A question I like to ask my brothers and sisters in Christ is this: "Are you a saint?" Well, are you? Most people respond that they realize that they're not perfect, but they do their best. And while this response may seem modest, it is wrong on so many levels and it is the kind of thinking that keeps us from full acceptance of the gift of our Father's grace. What in fact has He said in His Word? "You were cleansed; you were made holy; you were made right with God by calling on the name of the Lord Jesus Christ and by the Spirit of our God."[5]

Am I just making this up? Am I just picking and choosing what I want to believe about God's forgiveness for my own peace of mind?

But it was Jesus Himself who said, "Whoever believes in Him is not condemned, but whoever does not believe is condemned already, because he has not believed in the name of the only Son of God."[6] And the great apostle Paul reiterated this gospel. "Therefore, there is now no condemnation for those who are in Christ Jesus, because through Christ Jesus the law of the Spirit who gives life has set you free from the law of sin and death."[7]

We either believe God or we don't. We either accept His Word or we don't. He has made it abundantly clear that the sacrifice of Jesus was enough. Is not the grace of God Almighty sufficient to provide a cover for our sins? *Is not the work that Jesus our God accomplished on the cross enough for us?*

As a father, the work that I do serves as a blessing for my children. I get up early and labor and earn my pay so that my children will have what they need. The work that their father accomplishes is enough to provide for them. There is nothing that my children can do to add or take away from what I, their loving father, have done. Compared to me, they can't even begin to do the work that I do for them, and they couldn't come close to accomplishing for themselves what I can. Sure, they can squander the blessing. But the labor is mine, and the fruit of that labor is mine to share with them. Their job is not to match my efforts, but as loving and respectful children, their role is to honor me as their father and make good use of the fruits of what I have worked to earn for them. So you tell me: Is the work of Jesus on the cross enough, or are you under the illusion that somehow you are going to add or take away from the work of your Father in heaven?

HEALING

Coming face-to-face with the gospel and embracing forgiveness through the willing sacrifice of Jesus on the cross, we are invited not only into right standing with God but actual healing for our wounded souls. We read in scripture that there were real supernatural healings of people's bodies. People who had spent their entire lives blind were given sight to see. The lame walked, lepers were cleansed, and mysterious discharges were ceased, all by the mighty hand of God. And Christ promised to His followers that mightier works than these would be done in His name following His ascension to the Father.

These gifts of physical healings remain controversial to this day. There continues to be debate among the saints as to whether or not Christ still heals physically as He did when He was first establishing His church. In my own experience, I have witnessed divine healing. And to me, it is sufficient to say that Christ is the same yesterday, today, and forevermore. But the discussion is for another time. What I do *not* believe is up for discussion is whether or not Jesus continues to heal the soul. I believe that He undoubtedly does. And it's great that He does because it's this healing that opens our hearts to the love of the Father.

You see, Jesus promised that He would not leave us as orphans. He would send to us His Spirit. The Wonderful Counselor, the Comforter, the Spirit of Truth. According to Jesus, He would live with us and in us. The Spirit of God, the God of love, dwells within us. As Paul would say, "Do you not know that your bodies are temples of the Holy Spirit, who is in you, whom you have received from God?"[8] What this means is that within our very self resides the God of peace. Jesus promised that His peace He would give to us. His joy. And this peace and joy can only come by the working of His Holy Spirit. We're going to dive deeper into this later on in the book. But for now, we must appreciate that Jesus has gifted us His peace and joy and He has granted us healing of the soul by His own Spirit.

But what does that look like? Having lived life carrying around wounds of our past, how do we even know what it looks like to have these wounds healed? I believe we find the answer in the hearts of our children. In fact, it was Jesus who said that we must become like children if we are to receive the kingdom of heaven. And watching my own boys, I can see why.

Whenever my oldest son gets upset, he comes to me and hugs me. He cries into my shoulders. If he is really upset, he wails loudly into my ears. And as I hold him, I let him know that he's OK. I remind him that he is loved and squeeze him nice and tight in my arms. When he is ready, I pull away just enough to be able to look him in the eyes and assure him that he's OK. I gently wipe his tears away, give him a kiss, and tell him that I love him. When he's calm enough, I'll tickle him or play with him to make him laugh. It seems that no matter how upset he was, being embraced in my arms, reminded that I love him, and knowing for sure that I am here to protect him, he is able to smile again and overcome whatever it is that burdens a toddler's heart.

Please don't misunderstand. I don't want to trivialize serious trauma as if it somehow equates to whatever small things can bring a two-year-old to tears. What I want you to understand is that true healing comes in the embrace of the Father. It comes in knowing that He loves you with a love that is so fierce, that He would send His only Son to die for you. He would subject Himself to the anguish of seeing His Son murdered so that you could experience grace and peace with Him. True healing comes in believing who He says you are. He says that you are His child. He says that you are His own and that you bear His name. Healing comes from knowing that He is your protector. It comes in trusting that He is not only faithful and just to forgive, but He is faithful to complete the work He has begun in you and that He will work all things for the good of those who love Him and are called according to His purpose.

CHAPTER 3 REFLECTIONS

1. Have you accepted God's free gift of grace? Do you accept that Jesus's sacrifice has secured God's forgiveness over your life? If you're not sure, what is keeping you from doing so?

2. Have you experienced the healing that comes from accepting Jesus Christ into your heart? What is preventing you from doing so?

3. How does knowing that you are forgiven and receiving the healing power of the gospel change your relationship with God the Father?

Prayer Invitation

The scripture says that if we believe in our hearts and confess with our mouths that Christ is Lord, then we are saved. Do you believe in your heart that Jesus has paid the price for your sins? Do you believe that He has healed you? Pray that the Lord would reveal His grace to you in a powerful way. The gospel is the power of God to save. Pray that the Father would help you to experience that power. Pray that both your heart and mind would be convinced that you have indeed been forgiven by grace and that you have indeed been healed by the wounds of Christ. In Jesus's name. Amen.

CHAPTER 4

BORN AGAIN

Jesus replied, "Truly I tell you, unless someone is born
again, he cannot see the kingdom of God."
—John 3:3 (CSB)

We just got done discussing the healing and forgiveness that comes
through faith in Jesus Christ and the sufficiency of His sacrifice on
the cross. We are new in the eyes of God our loving Father, and we
walk into a new life with the peace and joy that He has gifted us
with His own Spirit. This newness of life is no little matter. It is part
of a profound and fundamental teaching that Christ discussed with
the religious leaders of His time. The reality of being "born again."

Spiritual rebirth is a concept that is unique to the Christian life.
The biblical interpretation of this concept is not just a reformation of
thinking or an adoption of new philosophies. Essential to walking
alongside God, according to Jesus, is that one must literally be
born again. In fact, Jesus's precise words were "Truly, I tell you
emphatically, unless a person is born from above he cannot see the
kingdom of God."[1]

This teaching of being born again is foundational to an
understanding of how a child of God comes to know his or her
Heavenly Father. Not too different from a physical birth, a spiritual
birth brings with it a process of nurturing, learning, and growing.

This process requires intentionality and humility. More often than not, as we've already discussed in previous chapters, we mistakenly apply our past life experiences as limitations to this process. If we are to live with childlike faith, we must become like children in how we walk with God.

THE BIRTH OF A NEW LIFE

The development of human life in the womb is fascinating. To this day, despite our many advances in the sciences, we do not fully comprehend the great mystery of the journey that human beings go through as they form in their mothers' wombs. I don't pretend to know all of the deep scientific details, but I am aware that at some point in a child's development, he begins to become aware of the world that exists outside of his humble home.

The womb is a dark place. Everything my sons experienced in the first part of their lives was clouded by the fact that they were not able to actually see what was responsible for the sounds they heard, the movement they felt, or the light that filtered in. Their experience was veiled by the walls in which they resided. Though their senses were somewhat alive, they were able to hear but not understand and see but not really perceive.

Despite what anyone may say, the child who resides inside his mother's womb, pressing against her abdominal walls, jumping and stretching, and reacting to her sounds, her emotions, and her movements is indeed alive. Yet the child has not yet fully experienced life. Until the day he is born, the child, though living, is not fully alive. He has not yet seen the light that shines in the day. He has not yet experienced fully the world of the living that waits for him outside her womb. What he has experienced thus far is only a shadow of the greater reality. And in similar fashion, such is the life of one who has spent his or her entire life having only experienced a physical birth and never having experienced the spiritual birth that comes through Christ.

When my first son was born, my first thought was *Finally!* From the moment I knew my wife was pregnant, I was so excited to meet my little man. I was so excited to hold him and love him. I watched him intently as the nurses bathed him, weighed him, and ensured that he was a healthy baby. All the while, he had no way of really recognizing me. He was exhausted from his journey through the birth canal. He spent most of the first two or three days of his life resting outside of that dark womb. His eyes were mostly closed, and he would only cry and open his mouth when he was near his mother's breast to feed. Disoriented and exhausted, he met me, his father, for the first time. But coming from such a dark place and entering such a new world, he did not yet fully understand and could not yet fully embrace the love of his father.

Much in the same way, being born again can be very disorienting for the baby Christian. Our spiritual birth is manifested by the Spirit of God. We come alive through the power of the Holy Spirit, leaving behind the dark womb that is life without the "Light of men." No amount of human effort can bring about a spiritual rebirth. This is because, as Jesus said, "Humans can reproduce only human life, but the Holy Spirit gives birth to spiritual life."[2] We often picture this birth as a beautiful process filled with the majesty of God's saving grace. But just like when a woman births a child, the spiritual rebirth does not come without its own labor pains. In fact, Jesus says, "Dear children, it is very hard to enter the Kingdom of God! ... Humanly speaking it is impossible."[3]

Too many of us perceive our spiritual rebirth as just an extension of our physical existence. We understand in our minds that we are a new creation in Christ, but in our hearts, we fail to realize that we have just been birthed out of a dark existence where the life we knew wasn't really living. We are born again on Sunday, and by Monday, we go on living as if the only thing that has changed about us is our religious preference. But the truth is that we often look just like my little boy when he was born; eyes only slightly opened, crying out for nourishment, exhausted and disoriented, we finally meet our Father for the first time. And because we often fail to take the time to really get to know Him, we run off into the world in that same disoriented state. But this should not be so. If the children of God are to be mighty warriors of the kingdom, they must learn to drink from the true Vine and grow in their understanding of the love of the Father first.

NOURISHMENT FROM THE FATHER

For some reason, even though we all know what dark place we came from before meeting Jesus, we take for granted the toll that our past life has taken on us. Because of this, when we come to saving faith, we jump right into service and work hard to become faithful members of our congregation. We are grateful to God, and we want to display that gratitude. However, we would never expect from a newborn child the kind of behavior we expect from ourselves when we are born again. Instead, we nourish the baby, comfort her, clean her, dress her, and spend hours, days, and weeks letting her get to know us. Knowing that she has just been introduced into a completely new life, we care for her and slowly build her up in the ways she should go.

If we then, who are evil, know how to be good to our children, how much more will our Heavenly Father know how to be good to us? If we know better than to send a baby out to do work on our behalf, doesn't the Father know this even more? What comes after the child is born? What comes after the excitement of a new life has passed and reality has set in? The child now communes with her parents, and she learns and grows in her understanding. Not only does she begin to see life in a new way, but she also begins to experience the love of her parents in a whole new way. Where before, the child received sustenance from her mother in a passive way through the umbilical cord, the child now has to be fed milk actively in order for her to live and grow. Her very life depends on her resting in her mother's arms and suckling from her nourishing breasts. Is it any wonder then that Peter writes to the believers (emphasis mine), "Like newborn infants, *long for the pure spiritual milk*, that by it you may grow up into salvation"[4]?

This longing for pure spiritual milk is no small matter. For the child of God, it is truly the difference between life and death. It is the difference between perceiving the love of the Father intellectually and *experiencing* the love of the Father in reality. We would never overlook the need of a newborn for milk. In fact, so serious is a child's need for sustenance, that when the mother is unable to produce adequate amounts of milk, artificial milk is used to ensure the baby is nourished. Praise God that our Father never runs out of sustenance for us! His are rivers of "living water" that never run dry. He tells us to hunger and thirst for righteousness and we will be satisfied. There is no need for us to seek out artificial milk! Instead, we are invited to seek out true food and true drink in Christ Jesus. We are invited to abide in the True Vine and to receive fully the love of the Father.

Mary understood this, didn't she? Mary recognized the good portion. She recognized that the best thing for her was to sit at Jesus's feet, to take in His words, and to hold them in her heart. She knew that in Him was life. Mary is a wonderful example for the newborn Christian to emulate. More than Paul, Peter, or James, I would argue that it is essential that the baby Christian observe the heart that Mary had for the sustenance that came from the presence of God. If we are to be fully convinced of the Father's love, if we are to grow from a newborn to a mature child of God, we must take to heart what Christ spoke before submitting Himself to the cross.

> I am the true vine, and my Father is the gardener. Every branch in Me that does not produce fruit He removes, and He prunes every branch that produces

fruit so that it will produce more fruit. You are already clean because of the word I have spoken to you. Remain in Me, and I in you. Just as a branch is unable to produce fruit by itself unless it remains on the vine, neither can you unless you remain in Me. I am the vine; you are the branches. The one who remains in Me and I in him produces much fruit, because you can do nothing without Me.[5]

WORKING FOR THE FATHER

But what about "the Great Commission"? What about spreading the gospel? What about "good works"? What about going forth and making "disciples of all nations, baptizing them in the name of the Father and of the Son and of the Holy Spirit, teaching them to observe everything [Christ has] commanded you?"[6] These are fair questions. To them I always respond with my own question. Whom has God ever sent without first revealing Himself to them and raising them to be His disciple?

He intervened on Moses's behalf when he was a child so that he would grow up and observe the travesties against God's people in Egypt. Once he was grown, God met him in the wilderness. And before Moses was fully convinced, the Lord showed Him displays of His power and revealed to him for the first time His wondrous name. David was a shepherd boy who witnessed the power of God long before he stood before Goliath. The disciples themselves communed with Jesus for three years before they witnessed His death and resurrection. And even then, before they could go out and preach the gospel outside of Israel, they were ordered to stay and wait for the promised Holy Spirit to come and give them power to labor on His behalf. In every instance, the people of God who committed magnificent works for the kingdom were first and foremost in intimate fellowship with God. And whenever the people of God attempted to act on their own assumptions about Him, they failed to glorify Him and ultimately fell into sin. The newborn Christian is no exception.

I did not make my children so that they would build my kingdom. I have plans that they will one day carry on my legacy, sure. I will raise them with a future hope that one day all that I have built for them they will steward. But I made them in order that I may love them. Because I love them, I will challenge them. There will be work to be done, so I, their loving father, will prepare them for that work. But before all of that, I will convince them that they are loved. They will not labor out of fear of punishment. They will not labor out of some misplaced sense of moral obligation. I will teach them to observe what Christ has commanded me. To love God with all my heart, with all my soul, with all my strength, and with all my mind. And to love my neighbor as I love myself.

We will discuss in a deeper sense the obligation we have to spread the gospel. I don't want you to close this chapter thinking for a second that we don't have an assignment as God's children to go forth and make disciples. In fact, that is why I want you to be convinced that you are loved by the Father. I want us to be like Christ who "knew that the Father had given everything into His hands, that He had come from God, and that He was going back to God."[7] So like Christ, I want us to make knowing the Father's love our number one priority. In doing so, we will be more than able to fulfill our God-given assignment of glorifying God by living out the gospel.

CHAPTER 4 REFLECTIONS

1. What does it mean to be born again? Have you been born again? How do you know?

2. What are you prioritizing in your walk with God? Getting to know Him more or working hard?

3. Why is it so important to get to know the person of Jesus? As a child of God, how are you investing in your relationship with Him? How can you get to know Him more?

4. How would knowing your Father's love more affect the way you approach your labor for the kingdom?

Prayer Invitation

Meditate on the reality that you have been born again. Thank the Lord that you are a new creation. Pray that He would help you seek intimacy with Him above all else. Ask Father God to help you get to know Him more. Accept His invitation to grow as a child of His and to engage intentionally in the process of development. Pray that He would continue to reveal more of His love for you and that He would lead you into the labor He has assigned for you to do to glorify Him. In the name of Jesus. Amen.

CHAPTER 5

GIVING HIS WORD

My son, be attentive to my words; incline your ear
to my sayings. Let them not escape from your sight;
keep them within your heart. For they are life to those
who find them, and healing to all their flesh.
—Proverbs 4:20–22 (ESV)

I have spent a lot of the early parts of my children's lives away from home. I watched my oldest spend his first birthday from across a phone screen. Though I would see him every so often via video chat, most of what he knew about me was what his mom could explain to him while I was away. As a small child, he couldn't really understand that the man in the photos was the man on the screen. And when I returned home, it was difficult for him to recognize that the man who had been on the screen was now the man standing in front of him. It seemed that for a child who was still learning to understand the world around him, it wasn't enough that someone would tell him about his father. He needed to actually spend time with his father himself.

In the same way, it is impossible to replace hearing from God Himself with discussions about God. Sermons, debates, discussions, and books like this one are no replacement for God's own words as revealed in scripture. The newborn Christian must learn to recognize his or her Father's voice by learning to hear Him when He's speaking. If our ears are clouded by the different sounds of different voices, we can be misled into following the wrong ones. Because we are called to grow from newborn infants in Christ, to mature laborers for the kingdom, we need to learn to go from the pure spiritual milk to the deeper meatier food. Therefore, I believe no conversation about growing in our experience of the love of the Father is complete without a conversation about the Word of the God.

THE AUTHORITY OF SCRIPTURE

Now before we get into what the Word of the God says, I am convinced we need to have a small conversation about what the Word of the God is. Concluding whether or not the Bible is truthfully God's anointed Word is crucial in whether or not we will get to experience the fullness of His love. The Bible is not only a collection of stories of God and His people. The Bible is the way in which He draws us to Himself, and it is the spiritual sustenance for His children. If we cannot come to terms with the fact that the Bible is God's inspired Word, we not only fall into deception and become susceptible to false teachings, but we also miss the opportunity to grow in our walk with God and to know our Father in a more meaningful way.

Consider what it would be like for a child who has spent his whole life separated from his father to find himself in a room full of men pretending to be his father. How would he be able to discern which one is his? It would be necessary for him to have some sort of reference to help him confirm whatever was being said to him. Birth certificates, identification, history of residence, etc. Without proper documentation, the child is forced to depend on his own feelings and on the words of men who may be intentionally or foolishly deceiving the child. Similarly, as children of God who were once separated from Him, we find ourselves bombarded with contradicting messages from people about who our Father is. In fact, one could argue that this book is another attempt to make up stories about the Father.

Because of this, we have to make a choice as to whether or not we believe that the sixty-six books of canon are actually reliable. We have to decide whether or not we trust them. I want to avoid turning this into an apologetics section, but I also want you to consider the importance of the matter. There are wonderful resources outside the scope of this book to address the all-important question of whether or not the Bible is true. I *highly* encourage you to seek them out. But for now, I want to talk about the implications of rejecting the authority of the Bible.

The Bible serves as a reference for the child of God. With so much information out there, one has to be able to discern what is reliable and what isn't. What happens when we *do* reject the authority of scripture? What happens to its message? Historically, when we reject the authority of the Bible, we replace it with a new and false "gospel." We replace the message of salvation by grace through faith with vain messages of works. Our purity becomes wholly dependent on ourselves. Our Father in heaven becomes far off and His love for us hangs on our ability to be faithful to Him. He is suddenly made in the image of man and not the other way around. We are the ones who have to save ourselves by our good works, our consistent church attendance, regular prayer, proper clothes, faithful adherence to liturgy, and on and on. When we reject the gospel that is given to us in the Bible, we take on a false gospel that has no power to save.

And Paul warned about this false gospel. Speaking to the Galatians who had been deceived into believing that they had to earn their salvation, he had this to say:

> I am surprised at you! In no time at all you are deserting the one who called you by the grace of Christ, and are accepting another gospel. Actually,

there is no "other gospel," but I say this because there are some people who are upsetting you and trying to change the gospel of Christ. But even if we or an angel from heaven should preach to you a gospel that is different from the one we preached to you, may he be condemned to hell! We have said it before, and now I say it again: if anyone preaches to you a gospel that is different from the one you accepted, may he be condemned to hell![1]

Seems a little harsh, doesn't it? However, what if it was *you* trying to get a message to your own child? How would you feel knowing that someone had perverted that message and misconstrued it to change what you had to say?

My wife, for example, writes a journal about the lives of our little boys. Each boy has his own dedicated journal. In those pages, she details not only the events that have taken place in their lives but also her own emotions behind them. She captures the love she has for them and tells them all that they mean to her. She hopes to one day share those journals with our sons. But what would happen if someone came and misconstrued her words? What if someone convinced our sons that she did not actually write those words? There would be a whole story of love that would be lost to them. Similarly, when God's children are convinced that His love letter is a forgery or that it isn't completely trustworthy, a gap is formed between His love and their hearts and minds. Thankfully, He is faithful to preserve His "journal" and we can and should trust that what He has preserved for us is reliable.

Again, there is plenty of information on the topic that you should definitely look into when you have the time. But I want you to also consider what the scripture says about itself. Peter wrote,

No prophecy of scripture comes from someone's own interpretation. For no prophecy was ever produced by the will of man, but men spoke from God as they were carried along by the Holy Spirit.[2]

Paul wrote to Timothy,

All Scripture is breathed out by God and profitable for teaching, for reproof, for correction, and for training in righteousness.[3]

He wrote to the Romans saying,

For whatever was written in former days was written for our instruction, that through endurance and through the encouragement of the Scriptures we might have hope.[4]

Jesus Himself spoke of the scriptures. He declared to the Pharisees,

You study the Scriptures diligently because you think that in them you have eternal life. These are the very scriptures that testify about me.[5]

Moreover, it is Jesus who said, "Scripture cannot be broken."[6] By now I hope the point is clear. We have to decide whether or not we believe the Bible. Not only to avoid its warnings but also to receive its blessings. The Bible is not only an instruction book for life. It is not just a collection of stories. The Bible is God's love letter. And if we are to come face-to-face with His love, we must accept His scripture as true.

THE BEAUTY OF GOD'S WORD

Coming to terms with the authority of God's Word isn't just about knowing the rules or what instructions to follow. God's Word is ultimately a beautiful expression of His love for His children. Knowing it, trusting it, and believing it is one very important way that His children come to know Him more intimately. The psalmist understood this. He wrote the longest chapter of the psalms about just how precious God's Word was to him. Celebrating in God's Word, he wrote,

> I rejoice in following Your statutes as one rejoices in great riches. I meditate on Your precepts and consider Your ways. I delight in Your decrees; I will not neglect Your Word.[7]

Many of my brothers and sisters in Christ consider the reading of scripture a moral obligation. Rather than viewing it as an opportunity to fellowship with God, we think of it a homework assignment that every faithful Christian must fulfill. We can get really hard on ourselves for failing to be consistent in our daily reading of God's Word. However, I challenge us to think about how it would affect our other relationships if we approached them with the same kind of attitude. What would my wife feel if it seemed that I only listened to her because I felt I had to? Not because I want to but because if I don't, I'll have to be nagged about it later. What about my children? What will I be communicating to them if it seems that every time they want to play, I concede because I feel that if I don't, I'm going to have to deal with the consequences later? Will I be fostering a relationship of love? Will I be growing in intimacy with my loved ones? Not at all. And I don't believe that our Father desires for us to treat His Word with that kind of attitude.

God's Word is a gift. More than just basic instructions before living eternally, it is one of the many important ways that our Father communicates to us daily. Christ, before surrendering Himself as the perfect sacrifice on the cross (in accordance with God's Word by the way), spoke this prayer to the Father over all of us. "Dedicate them to Yourself by means of the truth; *Your Word* is truth"[8] (emphasis mine). Think about that for a second. God the Son prayed to God the Father that He would dedicate His people to Himself by way of His Word! *What does that even mean?* It means that His Word is a means by which God draws us closer to Himself. By His Word, God shifts things within us. His Word is

> alive and active. Sharper than any double-edged sword, it penetrates even to dividing soul and spirit, joints and marrow; it judges the thoughts and attitudes of the heart.[9]

When we read His Word, we come face-to-face with a truth that tackles the lies that attack us daily. Past wounds, hidden sins, fears, doubts, emotional burdens, etc. In our Father's Word, we find the encouragement, the rebuke, the wisdom, and the perspective we need to grow in our love for Him and our trust that He is faithful to pull us through. Spending time in His Word is not about being a "good Christian." It's about spending time with Your Heavenly Father.

GOD'S WORD AS NOURISHMENT

God's Word is also meant to be nourishment for our souls. The human heart longs for sustenance that cannot be met with macro- and micronutrients. If we are being honest, many of us live with a full stomach but an empty heart. This is because we are not meant to "live by bread alone, but by every word that comes from the mouth of God."[10] We discussed in the previous chapter about being newborn children of God. Like a newborn babe, the young believer needs nourishment to grow his or her faith. There is no greater food for the child of God than His very life-giving Word.

When each of my boys was born, they relied exclusively on my wife's milk for sustenance. But every day, their nutritional requirements increased until they needed more than what their mother's milk could give them. We slowly began introducing soft foods. We watched them intently to make sure they could handle the texture and observed how they responded to the flavor. In their own time, they each began desiring more puree than they did their mother's milk. My youngest son actually weaned himself sooner than his brother because he wanted to eat what he saw his brother eating. When we perceived that they were ready, we began to feed them small pieces of food with tougher consistency. We started with small pieces of bread and then we began serving them scrambled eggs for breakfast and went from there until they were eating the same food we were. They each gagged at first. They were not accustomed to the new diet. But they needed it, and in time, they each desired more of it. Such is the way in which the child of God moves from first experiencing the Father's love to learning to "grasp how wide and long and high and deep is the love of Christ."[11]

For the child of God, the pure spiritual milk is the basic principles of the gospel. Recognizing our sin, accepting our need for repentance, understanding that Christ has paid for our sins— this is milk. Many of us are accustomed to being served milk on a regular basis. When we go to our weekend service or we attend our Bible study groups, there is a constant reminder that we are sinners, that Christ died for us, and that we need to repent from our sins and look to the cross. This is not a bad thing. However, as the writer of Hebrews states, "anyone who lives on milk, being still an infant, *is not acquainted with the teaching about righteousness*"[12] (emphasis mine). There is more to the gospel than Christ dying because we sinned. There are deeper implications about righteousness, more to know about the love of the Father. That's why I wrote this book! Because I want us to move beyond the elementary teachings about Christ and be taken forward to maturity, not laying again the foundation of repentance from acts that lead to death, and of faith in God, instruction about cleansing rites, the laying on of hands, the resurrection of the dead, and eternal judgment. And God permitting, we will do so.[13]

Moving from spiritual milk to meat is a process. As a loving father, I recognize that my sons cannot currently chew on a steak. Not only do they have difficulty chewing on that amount of meat, but the density of the food would also be too much for their little stomachs to handle. However, this does not mean that I allow them to rely on a liquid diet. I do not continue to feed them their mother's milk. Instead they eat pieces of shredded chicken. They are served mixed vegetables and chopped-up fruit. Some foods they can eat whole, and others they eat in smaller, bite-sized pieces. My oldest son can hold a sandwich in his hand and eat, while his younger brother needs us to tear off pieces for him. Day by day, they are exposed to heavier foods, heartier servings, and tougher consistencies. If I, who is evil, know how to lead my child from milk to solid foods, how much more does my Father in heaven know how to lead me from the elementary teachings of the gospel to increasing freedom and joy in the breadth and depth of His love?

And He takes us to these greater depths by feeding us His Word. Much like He did with Israel, He leads us through the wilderness, humbling us and teaching us to hunger for the manna He sent from heaven: Jesus. He shows us to hunger and thirst for righteousness that we may be satisfied in Him. He invites us to meditate on His Word daily that it may feed our souls and strengthen our bones! He invites us to "taste and see that the Lord is good!"[14] The more we feed on God's Word, the more His Spirit takes us from glory to glory, showing us the beauty of the Father's love. And the child of God needs this daily bread.

But after recognizing our need to spend time feeding our souls with God's Word, many of us will make time on our schedule to read the Bible even when we don't actually want to. However, God's Word should taste sweet to the soul. It should not only feed you like a nice serving of mixed vegetables; it should warm your heart the way your favorite dessert would. And I'm not saying you need to have an emotional experience every time you read scripture. But I *am* saying that you shouldn't be "eating" begrudgingly. If and when we find ourselves in that head space where our appetite is low and we're reading our Bibles because we think we have to or else, we should pause and contemplate why we're feeling that way. What distractions, what concerns, what fears, what ambitions, and what *anything* is getting in the way of our desire for God's true food? Much in the same way that we talk to our doctors when we have a decrease in appetite, we can always have an honest conversation with our Father about our decreasing desire to eat of His life-giving Word.

WRESTLING WITH OUR FATHER AND HIS WORD

Now more than not being in the mood to spend time in God's Word, there is a greater challenge that many believers face today. I have found that many of us feel that scripture is not reconcilable with modern times. There is a pressure to compromise what God has said in His Word in order to conform to the world or at least minimize the amount of friction that our fellowship with God might cause in our day-to-day. We rationalize away this compromise saying that some things don't apply anymore or that biblical times differ from modern times, so the Word of God doesn't need to be taken as seriously. I believe this is a huge disservice not only to us but to our Father in heaven.

We must realize something: we don't live under the Old Covenant (a.k.a. Old Testament) anymore, not because the Old

Covenant is irrelevant but because Christ fulfilled the righteous requirements of the Law. It is not that the Old Testament isn't valid anymore; it's that the Old Testament has fulfilled its purpose and made way for the New Testament or New Covenant. But you don't discard it like a dirty rag. It is evidence of God's faithfulness to His people. It is a testimony of His commitment to fulfilling His promises. We must realize that the promises that Christ has secured for us in the New Covenant, God spoke in the Old. How then can we know the fullness of what Jesus Christ has secured for us in His perfect sacrifice if we decide to dismantle God's Word and pick and choose the parts we like?

I believe that instead of undermining the authority of God's Word in its fullness, we are invited to wrestle with the parts that we don't quite understand, or we may not be ready to accept. I remember when I was first able to wrestle with my oldest son. It was a day I had been looking forward to ever since I was a big brother wrestling with my little sisters. I hoped that one day I would have my own children to play with. So I was excited to be able to tussle with my little man. And in the midst of that tussling, I received a profound revelation. Suddenly, the account of Jacob wrestling with God took on a deeper meaning for me.

My son charged at me with everything he had. He would dive head-on sometimes. He would yell and growl and grab at me and lay his entire weight on me. For fun, I would let him push me over and bring me to the ground. It made him feel strong, and it allowed us to actually play together. But whenever he was stuck beneath me, or whenever he couldn't stand up from a lack of balance, I grabbed him with so much ease and moved him to where he needed to go so we could continue our play. At any time, if I was actually trying to hurt him, I could have. But I restrained myself. For his sake. Just like God did with Jacob. Just like God does with us.

God seemed to have been restrained by Jacob. Yet He was able to with a simple touch of the hand to permanently displace Jacob's hip. He could have done this at any time, but He didn't. He restrained

Himself for the sake of Jacob's weakness. Similarly, I believe that our Heavenly Father invites us to wrestle with Him and with His Word. He gives us the freedom to doubt and question. To search out answers, to pour over the scriptures, to explore His creation, to interact with others who are made in His image. We are welcome to wrestle with what we don't understand. But we must remember that the truth is that His Word does not yield to us. No amount of wrestling with God's Word will lead us to be mightier than He. It would serve us well to accept God's Word humbly. To wrestle with our Father not as if we actually believe we will outsmart Him but humbly recognizing that He has the ultimate authority and power. In doing so, our grappling will lead us to a more genuine faith and a deeper understanding of the Father's love.

LOVING GOD'S WORD

If I could leave you with any advice about interacting with God through His Word, it would be that you learn to love His Word. I remember growing up with a strained relationship with my dad. I learned to despise most anything he had to say. Because of this, I would dismiss him whenever he would try to advise me. In the end, I endured many frustrations and disappointments that I could have avoided had I simply heeded his words. Now my father is not perfect. He made a lot of mistakes when I was growing up. But even he had my best interests at heart, and he meant well when he tried to advise me. If he, being evil, knew how to give wisdom and sound warnings, how much more does my Father in heaven know how to keep me from stumbling?

As the psalmist wrote, "Your Word is a lamp to my feet,"[15] so too I encourage us to see God's Word for what it is. Not only is it that lamp that keeps us from stumbling, but it is also a loving message from our Father; it is food for our souls. He is patient in His dealings with us. He understands that there are some things we just aren't ready to receive. But He wants to lead us from milk to solid food and invites us to wrestle with Him when we don't quite get it. So crack open your Bible and fellowship with your loving Father. Not as a homework assignment, and not like a spiritual diet, but like a child of God being attentive to your Father's words, inclining your ears to His sayings. Not letting them escape your sight, keeping them within your heart.

CHAPTER 5 REFLECTIONS

1. Does God's Word have full authority in your life? Why or why not?

2. What does God's Word mean to you? Is it a gift or a burden? Why a gift? Why a burden?

3. Are you living on milk, or are you allowing the Father to lead you to solid foods?

4. What are you wrestling with today?

5. How can knowing God's Word increase your awareness of the Father's Love?

Prayer Invitation

A prayer I believe the Lord is always happy to answer is the request that He would increase our love for His Word. If you find that your desire for His Word has waned, ask Him to increase your hunger and thirst for Him. When you open up the scripture, pray that He would not only grant you greater knowledge but that He would also reveal a deeper sense of His love for you. And as you tussle with meatier substance of scripture, pray that your Father would hold you throughout the process and that He would keep you from going too far to the left or right. Pray that God's Word would be implanted in your heart and that your soul would draw sustenance from it. In Jesus's name. Amen.

CHAPTER 6

GIVING HIS SON

We know that Jesus Christ the Son of God has come and
has shown us the true God. And because of Jesus, we
now belong to the true God who gives eternal life.
—1 John 5:20 (CEV)

Have you ever been told that you're just like your father or you're just
like your mother? Have you ever caught yourself speaking or doing
something and realizing, *Oh man, I'm becoming like my dad*? If you
have a good relationship with your parents, it may be a point of pride
when people tell you, "You're a chip of the old block." However, if
things aren't so good between you, you may hate the notion that "the
apple doesn't fall far from the tree."

For me, in spite of the struggles my dad and I faced as father and
son, I always wanted to be like him. I actually hated when people
told me I looked so much like my mom. I wanted people to look at
me and think of my dad. So it actually makes me smile when my
dad and I take photos together now and I really look like a younger
version of him. My wife and I laugh about the fact that when I quote
my dad in Spanish, it's like he entered the room. And there are so
many parenting choices that I make intentionally based off how my
father raised me. (Yes, even though our relationship was strained,
I have learned to appreciate certain things he did and taught me.)

My sons already remind us of each other. My parents tell me that my oldest son looks and acts just like I did when I was his age. My father-in-law tells us all the time that our little fireball, the youngest, reminds him of a little girl he once had running around in his own house. Children have a way of reflecting the personality and characteristics of their parents. Even children who may be estranged from them carry both biological and emotional markers that mirror the appearance and the personality of their mother and father. In an imperfect way, when we look at someone's child, we are seeing a little bit of them as well. When we look upon God the Son, however, we see the immaculate and awe-inspiring reflection of God the Father.

THE FATHER REVEALED

Jesus came to do so many things for us. He came to save that which was lost. He came to heal the sick, to encourage the poor, to preach the gospel, to die on the cross for our sins, and to rise again and overcome sin and death. The list really could go on and on. In fact, the apostle John tells us that there aren't enough books to contain all that Christ did while He was on this earth. However, I believe it can be argued that all that He did, everything I already listed and everything that can't be fully listed here, was ultimately part of the one thing He came to do: reveal the Father.

Jesus had many conversations with His disciples about many important matters of the kingdom of heaven. None, however, as important as the one He shared with them before being arrested and carried off to be crucified. The last words He spoke to them before He gave Himself up willingly on our behalf, He spoke so that we may all have peace in Him. It was in these final words where Jesus explained to His disciples.

> I am the Way, and the Truth, and the Life. No one comes to the Father except through Me. If you had

known Me, you would know My Father as well. From now on you do know Him and have seen Him.[1]

What a magnificent statement! In fact, it is these very words that led to my conversion. As a man who had been searching for truth, discovering that truth wasn't an idea but a person changed my life. And here, the Truth had spoken that He was the Way to life with the Father. Jesus is the eternal Son of God. He was the Word who was in the beginning with God. He is "the unique One, who is Himself God, [who] is near to the Father's heart. [And] He has revealed God to us."[2] And He has revealed God in a perfect way. So much so that when Philip asked Him to show them the Father, Jesus replied,

> Have I been with you all this time, Philip, and yet you still don't know who I am? Anyone who has seen me has seen the Father! So why are you asking me to show Him to you?[3]

All that Jesus did, everything He said, He did as a reflection of who the Father is. In fact, as He Himself put it,

> I tell you the truth, the Son can do nothing by Himself. He does only what He sees the Father doing. Whatever the Father does, the Son also does.[4]

It is my hope that my children will grow up to represent me well in the world. Not in an arrogant way but in a way that says that they and I have an intimate relationship with each other. I want their person and character to indicate to others who I am. What are my values, my priorities, and my quirks? Will meeting my children tell you about my sense of humor? Will getting to know them tell you how much I can love and how wisely I can teach? I pray to God that it does. Unfortunately, they face a challenge I know they will not be able to overcome on their own. They live in a world that is constantly vying for their attention and always trying to influence them. They will have family members, friends, teachers, and even strangers who will speak into their lives in ways that contradict my ways. Sin will attack their hearts and minds and cause them to stray away from my teachings. So even if I were a perfect father to them, which I most definitely am not, they would still not be a complete reflection of who I am. They would be a combination of what I pour into them and what the world does. But as I already mentioned, such is not the case with Jesus.

It is true that Christ faced many temptations when He walked as a man. Not only did Satan explicitly come and challenge His loyalty to the Father, but Christ also had to endure a barrage of criticism from family and friends, false teachings from religious leaders, social and political pressures from figures of authority, and the burden of walking in sinful flesh. "He was tempted in every way that we are. But He did not sin."[5] And this is so important because unlike my children, who will not be a perfect representation of me, and unlike me, who is not a perfect representation of my own father, Jesus is the perfectly faithful Son who represents His Father perfectly. There is no wrong in Him that can be found. So there is nothing in Him that isn't from the Father. When you look at Jesus, you are not seeing someone who allowed Himself to be influenced by outside forces. You are seeing someone who is in such perfect fellowship with His Father that He isn't just a "chip off the old block"; He is the whole thing! Therefore, if we want to fall deeper into the love of our Father, we must learn to fall deeper in love with His Son.

WHO IS JESUS CHRIST?

I once listened to a sermon given by the pastor at our local church where he discussed the importance of how we relate to people. He gave the imaginary example of someone who was passionate about his preaching and always sat at the front row during his sermons and he bought every book that he wrote. Then this imaginary person insulted one of the pastor's sons and showed contempt for them. The pastor asked us, "Do you think it would matter to me how much he claimed to love me if he treated my son that way? Do you think it would matter how many books he bought or how many sermons he attended?" Of course, no one hesitated to say that it wouldn't matter one bit. You can see how the same would be true about how we relate to God's only begotten Son—the One in whom He is well pleased.

What we think about Jesus is going to be the most important question in learning how to relate to Him. People have a lot of opinions about Him. Some people believe He is simply a prophet among prophets. Others believe He is one of many spiritual offspring of heavenly mother and father. Some even think of Him as a reincarnated angel. But the big question He asks is (emphasis mine) "What about you? … Who do *you* say I am?"[6]

We have to answer this question because it influences how we relate to Him, and as we already discussed, Jesus is supposed to be the One who reveals the Father to us. Our children and we cannot perfectly reveal our parents because that image has been marred by outside influences and by our own sins. As I'm sure you've already noticed, if you ask me about my own dad, you're going to get a skewed view of who he is. In other words, you're not going to get a completely accurate depiction of him. One might say that I could even mislead you to believe certain things about my father simply because I myself do not carry a clear picture in my heart of who he is. How dangerous is it then if we are to believe in a Jesus who isn't really the One who faithfully reveals the Father? Dangerous enough that the impersonator could mislead God's children to a false gospel and away from the Father's love.

Therefore, it is necessary for us to meet and know the One true Jesus as revealed in God's Word. Not the one who was spoken of on plates, not the one who was spoken of in a cave, not the one on any pamphlets. The One who is testified of throughout scripture. In

God's Word, Jesus says, "I am the Alpha and the Omega … the one who is, and who was, and who is to come, the Almighty."[7] When questioned by the high priest about His status as the Messiah, He responds, "I Am. And you will see the Son of Man seated in the place of power at God's right hand and coming on the clouds of heaven."[8] And perhaps most importantly, He says of His relationship to the Father and knowing Him, "No one knows the Son except the Father, and no one knows the Father except the Son and those to whom the Son chooses to reveal Him."[9]

So who is this Jesus? He is the eternal Almighty God. He is the anointed One who was promised to us all throughout the Old Testament. He is the Son of God who came to reveal to all of us the love of the Father. What does this mean for us? Is this just some deep biblical theology? Not. At. All. This is everything to us. This is why the gospel is the gospel!

Follow me here. If Jesus is anything but God, then that means that God remains distant from us. It means that God didn't come down personally to save His people. He remains separated from us, far from His people, too holy and righteous to commune with sinners. It means that instead of humbling Himself for our sake (as the scriptures say He did), He sent a mediator who is no different from any other prophet or messenger. No matter how much esteem you give Him, if He is not God, then God has not come close to you or me. But as it is, He is God. Again, as the apostle John put it,

No one has ever seen God. But the unique One, who is Himself God, is near to the Father's heart. He has revealed God to us.[10]

MEETING AND KNOWING JESUS

Once we wrap our heads around the person of Jesus, we must learn how we get to meet Jesus and how we can get to know Him.

Thankfully, this is actually quite simple. Jesus is the subject of the entire Bible. From the first letter to the last, all scripture points to Him. With that being said, there are definitely portions of scripture that point clearer to Him than others. For that reason, it is my recommendation that we begin where things are most clear—in the gospel accounts.

In fact, I think that's really part of the point of the gospel accounts. You see, without a focus on Jesus, the whole of scripture can be misunderstood or even manipulated. However, with Christ as the cornerstone of our understanding, as the foundation of our faith, we can help avoid such things. I always say that the farther away we get from the gospel, the farther away we get from the truth about the Father's love. So practically speaking, I believe a good practice is to read the four gospel accounts five times through. However, when reading them, do so not as a religious exercise; do it as if you're actually wanting to learn about the character of Jesus. Pay attention to the way He deals with people. Listen to His message. Did He preach, "Repent or go to hell"? Or did He preach, "Repent for the Kingdom of Heaven is at hand"?[11] Did He say to the woman caught in adultery, "Neither do I condemn you. Go and be free and act like this never happened"? Or did He say, "Neither do I condemn you. Go and sin no more"?[12]

Was Jesus a gentle pacifist who avoided conflict at all costs? Or did He flip the tables of the money changers in front of the temple and call out the religious leaders for their hypocrisy? Was He timid, or did He speak as One who had authority and look the rulers of His age in the face while proclaiming the truth of the kingdom? Did He come to condemn, or did He come to save? Was He concerned about political division, or did He say His kingdom was not of this world? The answers are there in scripture—in the four gospel accounts. And in everything we read the Son do, we are reading an expression of the Father's love.

When Jesus healed the sick, it was because the Father desires to heal us. When He rebuked lies and hypocrisy, it was because the Father desires our love to be true. When He spoke about the kingdom and saving sinners and how anyone who received Him received the Father, it was because the Father desires to rule in our lives and to restore our relationship with Him. So spend some time in Matthew, Mark, Luke, and John. Pay attention to the person of Jesus, and get to know the loving heart of God the Father.

Then, with Christ at the center of our faith and at the center of our understanding of God's Word, the whole of scripture comes alive with testimony of God's love. We read on in the New Covenant of the freedom that God's love brings through Jesus. We discover the power that we have to overcome sin in our own lives and of the unmerited favor we have received from God because of Jesus. We can appreciate our Father's righteous anger against sin and how He has always worked to protect His children in the Old Covenant until Jesus arrived. With the gospel of Jesus Christ as the lens through which we see God, we are no longer separated by our misunderstandings, our past hurts, or our own sins. We are now children of God brought closer to Him every day by the revelation of the Father through the person of His Son.

BECAUSE OF JESUS

Before moving on, I really want to emphasize the following: Because of Jesus, we can come to know the Father's heart. Because of Jesus, we can rest knowing that we are on good terms with God. Because "God made Christ, who never sinned, to be the offering for our sin, so that we could be made right with God through Christ."[13] Because of Jesus, we can come before God boldly in prayer. Because of Jesus, "all of God's promises have been fulfilled in Christ with a resounding 'Yes!'"[14] Because of Jesus, we know the true love of God the Father. "This is love: not that we loved God, but that He loved us and sent His Son as an atoning sacrifice for our sins."[15] Because of Jesus, we have a new life. No longer do we need to obsess over who we *were*, but we can move forward every day to who we *are* in Christ. We can move beyond the elementary teachings of repentance from sins and go into the beautiful discovery of a new life with God the Father, "being transformed into His image with ever-increasing glory."[16]

It is not because of you. It is not because of me. It is not because of this book. It is not because of any ministry, teaching, or web series. It is not because of your good works or mine. It is not because of all of our prayers. It is not because of our rule following. It is not because of our intelligence, our strength, or our personality. It is because of Jesus.

CHAPTER 6 REFLECTIONS

1. Who do you say Jesus is?

2. Why is knowing who Jesus is so important?

3. What do you see about the Father's heart when you look at Jesus?

4. How can knowing Jesus more intimately help you in your intimacy with God the Father?

5. Do you see Jesus throughout scripture? Why or why not? How can seeing Him through every page change the way you view God's Word?

6. Do you rest in the fact that Jesus is the reason we can come to know God, or do you burden yourself with the task of attempting to add to what Christ has already done?

Prayer Invitation

I am convinced that Jesus Christ is the greatest gift that God the Father has ever given us. And I am convinced that the whole reason He was sent was to reveal the love of the Father. Pray then that God would reveal Himself to you through Jesus Christ. Pray that when you read the gospel accounts you would be given eyes to see the work of the Father and ears to hear the voice of the Father. Pray that the Word would come alive with revelations of who Jesus is and who you are in Him. In Jesus's name. Amen.

CHAPTER 7

GIVING HIS SPIRIT

Therefore if you, being evil, know to give good gifts to
your children, how much more will the Father who is in
heaven give the Holy Spirit to those asking Him!
—Luke 11:13 (BLB)

As a father, I strive to do all I can for the good of my children. But
the love I have for them is not found in the roof over their heads, the
clothes on their backs, or even the food in their bellies. The love I
have for them is seen most in the fact that I am present with them.
What would it matter if I gave them the whole world and they never
had me with them to enjoy it together? Would there be any gift that
I could offer my children that would replace their need to be in the
loving presence of their father? I know it never mattered much that
my dad had bought us a nice house and that we had nice cars and
nice things. All that never replaced the emptiness of not having a
close intimate relationship with my father. But God does not show
His love by merely giving us things. He shows us His love by giving
us Himself.

God gave Himself to us when He sent God the Son to redeem
us from sin and to reveal to us God the Father. He didn't send
more prophets, angels, or any other kind of messengers. He came
down Himself as Immanuel—God with us. And when God the Son

ascended into heaven to sit at the right hand of God the Father, He sent God the Holy Spirit that we might know that we are His. Not satisfied to send anyone else on His behalf, God sent Himself so we might experience once and for all the eternal love of the Father.

THE TRIUNE GOD

Before we move any farther, I feel it is necessary to address a rather complicated but important topic. That is the topic of the triune nature of God. I don't want to get bogged down in a deep theological discussion, but I do think that it is important that we address this here.

Recall that Jesus came to reveal the Father to us. Before His time, there was only so much that people understood about the nature of God. But when Christ came, He presented a peculiar reality to us all. In His time on earth, Jesus showed that He was God. He talked about having authority over life and death, He displayed this authority in His resurrection, and He even ascribed to Himself the holy name of God. Yet He prayed to the Father often and spoke of Him as someone who was greater than He. It was the Father who sent Him, and it was the Father who worked through Him. Is Jesus Christ God the Father? No. Jesus Christ is God the Son, and He revealed God the Father.

God the Son also spoke to us about God the Holy Spirit. So venerated is the Holy Spirit that while blasphemy against the Father and the Son would be forgiven, blasphemy against God the Spirit would not. Jesus spoke of Him as the Spirit of Truth who would give us all that is from the Son and the Father. Echoing what the Lord God said to Ezekiel, He said, "I will put my Spirit in you and move you to follow my decrees and be careful to keep my laws."[1] Jesus tells His disciples that the Holy Spirit would be our Teacher and Counselor. God the Holy Spirit would remind us of everything that God the Son said and did on behalf of God the Father. And in the end, Christ commanded us to make disciples of all nations and to baptize not only in the name of the Son but in the name of the Father and of the Holy Spirit.

So when I say that God gave Himself for us and gave Himself to us that we might know Him fully, I am saying that God the Father sent God the Son, who sent God the Holy Spirit. From beginning to end, experiencing the love of God is an act of God. It is this fact that makes the gospel so powerful and so personal. It is why it is so important that we experience the love of the Father in the way He intended us to experience, by living in fellowship with the Holy Spirit.

WHO IS THE HOLY SPIRIT?

If we're going to embrace the love of God, we must meet and know the One who makes it all possible: the Holy Spirit. Firstly, it cannot be stressed enough that the Holy Spirit is a person, not a thing. He is a "He" and not a "what." He is the third person of the Holy Trinity of God. Like God the Son, Holy Spirit was present "in the beginning." It was He who moved over the void that existed before creation began. He came upon Mary conceiving God the Son in human form. He came upon Jesus, anointing Him for His mission on the earth. And He is a promised gift for all of God's children as a confirmation of our adoption as sons and daughters. He is God, and He is the One who "bears witness with our spirit that we are children of God."[2]

The Holy Spirit is the reason Christianity is not just a religion that you practice to make you feel better or to conform to social norms. He is the reason that knowing God the Father is not an exercise of the mind but a living relationship in the heart and soul. In the same way that the gospel is not true without Jesus being God the Son, the gospel is not true in our lives without God the Holy Spirit dwelling with us and in us. This is because the Holy Spirit confirms to us what Jesus preached when He said that the kingdom was at hand. God has "identified us as His own by placing the Holy Spirit in our hearts as the first installment that guarantees everything He has promised us."[3] Without the Holy Spirit, everything we are talking about in this book and reading in the scriptures is just ideas, philosophies, and religious theory. But if the Holy Spirit dwells within us, then "the Kingdom of God has come upon [us]."[4]

Think about it for a second. The entirety of the gospel is about how God so loved the world that He gave *Himself* for us. He gave His only begotten Son, and if

> while we were God's enemies, we were reconciled to Him through the death of His Son, how much more, having been reconciled, shall we be saved through His life![5]

This life that Paul writes about is found in God the Holy Spirit. It is in the reality that God comes to live with us, that He gives Himself as our eternal gift, and that we begin to *experience* the love of the Father and not just think about the love of the Father.

Even now, as you read this book, the Holy Spirit dwells with you. He is not far off, waiting to be summoned; He is *in* you, bringing new life and new perspective to your heart and mind. Do you think it is your natural ability to contemplate the things that are from above? Absolutely not! The Word of God states, "The one who is from the earth belongs to the earth, and speaks as one from the earth. The One who comes from heaven is above all."[6] It is not you or me who has the ability to discern the things of God. Again, it is not by human will that we enter the kingdom, and it is not by human will that we come to know the Father's love. It is the Holy Spirit who "searches all things, even the deep things of God."[7] In fact, apart from the Holy Spirit, we cannot even begin to perceive the things of our Father. There is a clear distinction between the mind of Christ and the mind of the flesh.

> Those who live according to the flesh set their
> minds on the things of the flesh, but those who
> live according to the Spirit set their minds on the
> things of the Spirit.[8]

If it is at all possible that we set our mind on the love of God the
Father, it is because God the Holy Spirit has made it so.

Another beautiful truth about the Holy Spirit is that He is a
witness of everything God has ever said, done, and plans to do. He
brings "power from on high" so that we can all testify of the freedom
that is found in Jesus Christ. He puts the words of the Father on our
lips; He seals the truth of Jesus in our hearts. He is the One who
spoke to the writers of scripture long ago, to record the history of
the Father's love. "For no prophecy was ever produced by the will
of man, but men spoke from God as they were carried along by the
Holy Spirit."[9] So when we read the Word of God and find that our
minds are being opened to the love of God, it is because the Holy
Spirit, the One who helped author scripture, is teaching us and
awakening our hearts to the Father's love. He is the reason we can
read scripture as a love letter from our Father in heaven. He is the
reason we can share this love with those around us.

Last and most definitely not least, the Holy Spirit is the One
who brings to us the presence of God. This should be obvious by
now, but I want to emphasize it. There can be many understandings
about the presence of God, and some can be very charismatic and
others not so much. However, regardless of the interpretation, it is
important to know that the Holy Spirit *always* brings with Him the
presence of God. We may not always be aware of it or sensitive to
this fact, but it is always true. If you are a child of God, then your
adoption is confirmed by the indwelling of the Holy Spirit and
therefore you are always in the presence of God. Failing to remember
this is part of what leads to insecurity and feeling like your Father
in heaven is distant.

Feeling your Father's presence is a beautiful thing. But depending on that *feeling* can be harmful to your trust in His love. I don't always get to be with my kids, so my presence isn't always with them. But even then, my love is always for them. However, God's presence *is* with His children always by His own Spirit. It is for this reason that we can "come boldly before the throne of grace" at any given time. It is because of the Holy Spirit that we need not doubt God's love for us. As the apostle John wrote,

> This is how we know that we belong to the truth and how we set our hearts at rest in His presence: If our hearts condemn us, we know that God is greater than our hearts, and He knows everything … And this is how we know that He lives in us: We know it by the Spirit He gave us.[10]

BORN OF THE SPIRIT

Did you know that a lot of who you are as a person is determined by your DNA? Not just your physical appearance but even your personality and how your body responds to environmental factors. Now there continues to be debate about the extent to which our genes determine our character traits, but there is a general consensus that they certainly play a significant role. And this makes sense when we consider that our DNA is the information that directs all of the cellular activity in our body and the formation of everything from the tips of our toes to the cells in our brains.

Personally, it blows my mind to think that running throughout my sons' bodies, deep within their DNA, is a piece of me. Literally half of their genetic makeup comes from me. Wherever they go, whatever they do, they will always have some of me with them. Not just as a memory of me or in some abstract way but in a very tangible and physical sense. Growing up, they won't realize that a lot of their behaviors are going to be not only because of our interactions with each other or because of their ideas of me but because of the way their DNA drives their development. They will have certain personality traits and be prone to certain emotional responses and thought patterns, partly because of the fact that they carry the DNA of their father. In the same way, the child of God lives out his or her life in a way that shows parts of who their Heavenly Father is because they carry within them part of His "DNA." They carry within them His Holy Spirit.

We've already talked about being born again as something that begins a process—a process of spiritual growth and development for the newborn child of God. A new creation is born, a new life that requires nurturing from the Father. But what exactly does it mean to be "born of the Spirit"? More than just a process, being born of the Spirit has everything to do with our newfound identity in Christ. It is about having new "DNA" that drives your character, your mindset, your behavior, and ultimately everything that you are.

According to Jesus, "That which is born of the flesh is flesh, and that which is born of the Spirit is spirit."[11] In other words, someone who is a newborn child of God is something completely different from what they were before. If you could somehow dissect the spirit of a child of God, you would see within their "genes" evidence of Jesus. In fact, it is no longer us who live but Jesus who lives within us. It is because of this that life and everything in it is completely different. And it is so important that we understand this if we are to walk in the freedom of the Father's love. Life is completely different for the child of God because the new creation is nothing like the old. It is not just a mixture of skin and bone. It is not just a combination of human DNA. The child of God is something new entirely. In fact, the scripture *explicitly* states, "If anyone is in Christ, the new creation has come: The old has gone, the new is here!"[12]

It is for *this* reason that we *must* move beyond the "elementary teachings" that we discussed in chapter 4! How can we, being no longer of the flesh, continue to contemplate the love of the Father from a fleshly perspective? Why are we so *obsessed* about who we once were when Christ Himself, the One who came and gave His life for us, has spoken that we are no longer who we once were. It is He who said, "If the Son sets you free, you are truly free."[13] And it is He who said, "Already you are clean because of the word that I have spoken to you."[14] And that is why Paul could write to the church in Corinth regarding the unrighteous who would not see the kingdom of heaven (emphasis mine), "Such were some of you. *But you were washed, you were sanctified, you were justified in the name of the Lord Jesus Christ and by the Spirit of our God.*"[15]

So let us take Paul's example and no longer regard Christ from a worldly perspective. From this constant place of dread and shame for our past lives or bitterness from our past hurts. Instead, let us look upon Him with new eyes. Eyes granted to us by the Spirit of God. Eyes that see that His work on the cross is finished and as such, we have been born again, by the Spirit, as children of our loving Father in heaven. Let us embrace His love knowing fully that we are His. Not sort of His. Not His but with some of the world in us. No. By His will, He has made us His own. By His Spirit, He calls us sons and daughters of God.

FELLOWSHIP WITH THE HOLY SPIRIT

As a father who loves spending time with his children, I wish I could spend all my days with them. I do wish I never had to leave to go to work. I wish every day was like a vacation day where I am up before them, waiting for them to wake up, preparing breakfast for them, and looking forward to spending all day together. Instead, I have to say goodbye to my children so often that whenever they see me grab my keys, they immediately yell out, "Bye, Dada!" They're just so used to seeing me leave. It doesn't mean I don't love them. God *knows* I do. It's just that I can't be with them all the time. Thank God that He *can* be with us all the time through the presence of His Holy Spirit.

I already mentioned that the Holy Spirit brings with Him the presence of God. Now this is not just a theological point. This is a reality for the children of God that means that they can fellowship with God daily. This is why you often hear Christians talk about "walking with the Lord." Because quite literally, Christians walk with the Lord wherever they go. Unfortunately, many of us, myself included, can take this fact for granted. Like teenagers who feel they're forced to hang out with their uncool parents, Christians can sometimes live out their lives as if being able to fellowship with God is no big thing. But it is *everything!*

Flip through the pages of scripture. From page one, God does amazing things. He brings something out of nothing, He brings light into the darkness, and He creates order out of chaos. God is the One who planted humankind in paradise; He walked among us in the beginning. He fought tirelessly against corruption; He made promises and fulfilled every single one. He disciplined His people, He rebuked them, He encouraged them, He healed them, and He led them. God humbled Himself completely to walk among us, and He let Himself be carried away to be abused for the sake of those who abused Him. He gave Himself willingly on our behalf that we may know Him fully. And now, *that* God, the One whose history with humankind is recorded for all to enjoy, God walks with you and me today. Literally.

Therefore, let us embrace this great gift that is God the Holy Spirit. Let us recognize that God Himself is with us and that we can fellowship with Him daily. He gave Himself to us completely. He has made us right in His eyes, and by the power of His own Holy Spirit, we are born again. Let your mind be renewed by Him. Recognize that He is in your "DNA" and that your character is more of who He is and less of who you were. Because of this, rest in knowing that you are loved completely by your Father in heaven. "May the grace of the Lord Jesus Christ, and the love of God, and the fellowship of the Holy Spirit be with you all."[16]

CHAPTER 7 REFLECTIONS

1. Look back to Luke 11:13. Having read this chapter, how do you understand that verse today? Has contemplating who the Holy Spirit is helped you understand just how deep the Father's love for you must be if He is willing to give Him to you as a gift?

2. Do you accept that you are a new creation, or do you continue to carry the burden of your past life? What keeps you from embracing who God says you are?

3. How often do you pause to acknowledge that God is with you? How can doing this more frequently and with more intentionality change the way you experience God's love?

4. How can you fellowship with God today? What can you do to invest in your relationship with the Holy Spirit?

Prayer Invitation

Today I invite you to pray that God would increase your awareness of His great gift, the Holy Spirit. Pray that He would make you sensitive to His presence in your everyday life. Pray that the Lord would awaken your senses to the fact that He is with you in a very real way. Pray that the Holy Spirit would convince you of the Father's love for you. Pray that whatever obstacles remaining in your heart, keeping you from resting in His presence, are removed in the name of Jesus. Amen.

CHAPTER 8

GIVING HIS KINGDOM

Fear not, little flock, for it is your Father's good
pleasure to give you the kingdom.
—Luke 12:32 (ESV)

My dad has always been a hardworking man. If there is any memory
I have of him, it's of him working diligently. Whether he was lifting
boxes in a warehouse, delivering heavy packages throughout the
city, driving the interstate, building things around the house, doing
landscape projects, or anything else, my dad was working hard.
He always talked about leaving me an inheritance. To this day,
even after I have my own family and have long been away from my
parents' home, he continues to talk about the inheritance he is trying
to secure so that he can leave it for me when he passes.

Now that I'm a father myself, I understand where he is coming
from. I see my little men and want all that I have to be theirs one day.
I want to leave an inheritance for them that their children's children
can enjoy. I want the work that I do in this life to be work that sets
them up for success. I don't want them growing up insecure about
their future. I want to have something for them to look forward to.
And while they're growing up, I am training them up to be ready to
steward all that I have for them in their inheritance.

I do not believe that this idea of a father wanting to leave an inheritance to his children is a cultural idea. I believe it is a sentiment that is ingrained into our hearts as human beings made in the image of our Creator. The Lord created man in His image and then gave us the heavens and the earth for us to steward and enjoy. He tasked us with being fruitful and multiplying so that our children's children would be able to also relish in God's inheritance. We know that this gift was lost when Adam and Eve chose to disobey the Lord. Praise the Lord that Jesus came to save that which was lost. He came preaching a wonderful message that was reminiscent of God's heart way back when He first created an inheritance for us in the Garden. He came preaching, "Repent! For the Kingdom of Heaven is at hand."[1]

THE KINGDOM

Heaven is real. It is a place. A place in which God sits enthroned as King and His dominion and authority is felt throughout. A place where He is not opposed by rebellious sin. Where angels bow and cry out "'Holy, holy, holy is the Lord God Almighty,' who was, and is, and is to come."[2] It is where God reigns supreme as King of kings and Lord of lords. The kingdom where peace and joy are found forever in His presence. It is a kingdom that, as God the Son explained, is "not of this world."[3]

And while the kingdom of heaven is not an earthly kingdom, there can be no doubt that God's authority to rule over this earth is eternal. No one can take away from God His right to rule. What *was* taken away was humankind's ability to live in peace under the rule of God as King. Like an angry teenager who rebels against the rule of his parents, humankind has spent history at odds with God's Kingship. Though we live day in and day out under His mercy and provision, we in our sinful state rebel against the authority of God and spend our lives trying to amass kingdoms of our own. From the moment Adam and Eve were fooled into believing they could be like God, humankind has struggled to attain his own kingdom apart from God. The consequence of this has been separation from our Father in heaven and hearts that lash out against one another in an effort to appease the hurt that comes with that separation. Thankfully, our loving Father has never been content to allow us to wallow in our own rebellion. He has always been at work, ensuring that the broken relationship between Him and His children would be restored. God would once again rule His people with wisdom and righteousness, and they would live in peace and joy in His presence. No longer would His children be insecure, and no longer would they destroy each other as a result of that insecurity. His kingdom would come, and His will would be done on earth as it is in heaven.

Now while the story of the kingdom is found throughout scripture, the concept is introduced to us in Genesis when the Lord makes His covenant with Abraham. He said to Abraham, "I will make you very fruitful; I will make nations of you, and *kings* will come from you. I will establish my covenant as an everlasting covenant between me and you and your descendants after you for the generations to come, to be your God and the God of your descendants after you"[4] (emphasis mine). Look at the Father's heart! It was His good pleasure to bless Abraham with this promise and to establish a relationship with those who would come after Him. Notice He said that kings would come from Abraham. These kings would be meant to rule over God's people on His behalf and with His guidance and wisdom.

We see this intent from God in Exodus after the Lord had called Israel out of Egypt and they stood at the foot of Mount Sinai. The Lord gave His people three days to prepare, then on the third day, He appeared before them on the mountain as proof that all they were about to receive was from God Himself. This would be the moment when God's people would receive His Law for the first time. Their covenantal relationship would be inaugurated with the sprinkling of sacrificial blood over the people. It was here where the Lord first said to His people, "You will be for Me a kingdom of priests and a holy nation."[5] These words were later echoed by the apostle Peter when he wrote, "You are a chosen people, *a royal priesthood, a holy nation*, God's special possession, that you may declare the praises of Him who called you out of darkness into His wonderful light"[6] (emphasis mine). In other words, it has always been in God's heart to rule among His people as King with them as His holy nation. It has always been His good pleasure to give you and me the kingdom.

THE KINGDOM OF HEAVEN IS LIKE ...

In my house are many rooms. When my children hunger and thirst, there is a room where they find the nourishment they desire. My children have a place to find rest for their weary souls. They are free to roam around and play throughout the living room. When they are upset, they can always find us in any room for comfort and peace. When they seek, they find. When they knock, it is opened to them. When they ask, they receive. They don't realize it yet, but everything they could need, my wife and I are able to provide for them. And that is by the grace of God.

Now my resources are very finite. This means that while I may have an abundance, what I have to give them is not eternal. There is a natural limit to what I can provide my children. Even still, I am more than happy to work hard and provide for them in the ways that I can. I am thankful to the Lord for the strength and opportunities to be able to give my children a place where they can dwell in the joy and peace of my love. But I do not own a kingdom. I have no kingdom of any kind to gift my children. I may want to give my children good gifts, but my Father in heaven has *much* more to give them. He wants to give all of us His kingdom!

But what does that even mean? What does that look like? Many of us have never lived in a kingdom. Most of us have learned that kingdoms are dreadful places where kings rule with injustice and the little man gets the short end of the stick. It seems that yet again, our previous understanding of things stands in the way of what it is God our Father is wanting to do for us. How then can this be something we look forward to? How can we relate to this promise of the kingdom of heaven? Or as Jesus said, "What shall we say the kingdom of God is like, or what parable shall we use to describe it?"[7]

Firstly, the kingdom of heaven is eternal, and its worth is immeasurable. Its value is not volatile, and it cannot be touched by the condition of the local or even global economy. If there *were* a way to buy it, it would be "like a merchant in search of fine pearls, who, on finding one pearl of great value, went and sold all that he had and bought it."[8] Picture, if you will, the greatest image you can of what you consider to be financial prosperity. The kingdom of heaven is worth more than that. Take every single cent that has been spent on this earth since forever. The kingdom of heaven is worth more than that. People are often impressed by each other's wealth. There are people who are held in high esteem simply because they have money. But no amount of material wealth on this earth will ever amount to what is the value of the kingdom of heaven. The merchant is wise to sell everything he has if it will buy him such a great pearl.

Does this mean that as children of God we will be granted financial prosperity? Not exactly. It's actually better than that! It means that as a child of God, you no longer labor as someone who is worried about what they eat, what they will drink, or what they will wear. You don't have to serve money anymore and worry that you might not have enough. "These things dominate the thoughts of unbelievers, but your heavenly Father already knows all your needs. Seek the kingdom of God above all else, and live righteously, and He will give you everything you need."[9] We can be confident of this because "He who did not spare His own Son, but delivered Him over for us all, how will He not also with Him freely give us all things?"[10] Having been gifted the kingdom of heaven, we have access to *every* provision that we would ever need.

With that being said, we must be careful not to become presumptuous or entitled. We need to learn to find the balance between the prodigal son and his older brother. We can't be so greedy that we would come to our Father and essentially ask to have our inheritance without having to have Him attached to it. That is what the young man did. Rather than live in peace under his father, he chose his father's wealth and went off to squander it without him. But we must be careful not to be like the older brother either. He was so wrapped up in laboring faithfully for the father that he forgot something very important about his father's heart. "You are always with me, and all that is mine is yours."[11] If we can rest in the reality that we serve the Lord, we can be confident that no work that we do will go unpaid or uncelebrated.

There is so much more to say about the riches of the kingdom. However, I don't want to overwhelm you with it. What I will say is that sometimes it seems as if this particular promise of provision isn't true. Some of you may be reading this and be dealing with physical hunger. You might have bills you can't pay. You might be praying for a job or an opportunity in order to provide for your family. At times like those, you're not so sure it's true that you are worth more than the birds of the air. To you I say, "Take heart. God has not abandoned you, and He has not forgotten to provide for you." If you're reading this book now, it is only because He wants to remind you that in spite of the given circumstances, you remain under His watchful eye.

It's true that sometimes we find ourselves in situations in which our own mistakes have led to our downfall. Like the apostle James says, "You don't have what you want because you don't ask God for it. And even when you ask, you don't get it because your motives are all wrong—you want only what will give you pleasure."[12] But other times, we find ourselves in circumstances because God is wanting to refine our faith. He *entrusts* us with trials. He knows that suffering "produces endurance, and endurance produces character, and character produces hope, and hope does not put us to shame, because God's love has been poured into our hearts through the Holy Spirit who has been given to us."[13] So take heart and know that He is with you even now. Keep your eyes and ears open to the provisions He has made so far, and remember that He will always make a way for you.

This brings us to another aspect of the kingdom. It is a kingdom that is ever advancing. In heaven, the will of God is done just as He desires it to be. All who dwell with Him honor and revere His holy name. Peace is maintained in His wonderful presence. But this is not the case on earth. Not yet. But Jesus told us to pray this famous prayer: "Our Father which art in heaven, Hallowed be Thy name. Thy Kingdom come. Thy will be done in earth, as it is in heaven."[14] And it does come! In fact, the kingdom is at hand! But this happens not quite in the way many of us expect it. Jesus said, "The coming of the kingdom of God is not something that can be observed, nor will people say, 'Here it is,' or 'There it is,' because the Kingdom of God is in your midst."[15] It may be that the newborn child of God doesn't even realize that he or she is living in the kingdom already!

Remember that the kingdom of heaven is the place in which God rules. Well, for the children of God, this place is in our hearts. Now again, heaven is still a real place that is not here on earth. But while we wait for the day we get to live in perfect peace in that place, the kingdom has come down to us! When Jesus was being accused of casting out demons by the prince of demons, He rebukes His critics and says, "If I drive out demons by the finger of God, then the Kingdom of God has come to you."[16] It is by the Holy Spirit that Jesus drove out demons. It is this same Holy Spirit who brings to us all that is from God the Father and God the Son. Therefore, He brings to us the kingdom of heaven as well! He brings to us the peace and comfort of knowing God. He brings to us the Law of God and works within us to obey this perfect Law of love so that God is honored as holy in our lives. But again, this is a process. It takes time. Like mixing yeast into tons of dough or like planting a small mustard seed that grows into a massive tree, the coming of the kingdom of heaven takes time.

Now sometimes as the kingdom advances in our lives, we

can misinterpret events as a series of punishments and rewards. Punishments for bad behavior and rewards for staying in line. But nothing could be farther from the truth. Instead, the coming of the kingdom is a matter of tasting and seeing that the Lord is good and about being "transformed by the renewal of your mind, that by *testing* you may discern what is the will of God, what is good and acceptable and perfect"[17] (emphasis mine). When you finally come to a place where you seek first the kingdom of God, you will experience "the Father ... grant[ing] you to be strengthened with power through His Spirit in your inner being, so that Christ may dwell in your hearts through faith—that you, being rooted and grounded *in love*, may have strength to *comprehend with all the saints what is the breadth and length and height and depth, and to know the love of Christ that surpasses knowledge, that you may be filled with all the fullness of God*"[18] (emphasis mine). So let us be encouraged that as the kingdom comes, the ups and downs we may experience are part of the process of growth. The farther the kingdom advances in our lives, the more we discern the will of God and the greater our appreciation and peace in the love of our Father.

In regard to the advancement of the kingdom, there is an important aspect that Christ discussed that I have seen become a stumbling block for many believers. I'm not sure why this happens, but it does seem to happen often, and I know it's happened to me. I'm talking about the fact that as the kingdom grows in our midst, because it often doesn't do so in the way we expect it, we can become very hypercritical of ourselves and of others. We lose our focus on Jesus, we forget to rest in the love of the Father, and we become very judgmental in a not so godly way. We take it upon ourselves to preserve the holiness of God's church as if we're not convinced that Christ meant what He said when He declared, "I will build My Church; and the gates of hell shall not prevail against it."[19] So rather than be invested in our relationship with our Father, trusting that "He who began a good work in you will carry it on to completion until the day of Christ Jesus,"[20] we spend our time on the lookout for the false believers, the false teachers, the false prophets, and the false everything. Rather than focusing on the truth of the gospel and the kingdom come, we overwhelm ourselves with the undue burden of trying to differentiate between the wheat and the chaff. But this should not be so.

That kind of behavior, the obsession with making sure the "right people" are among you, is not what the kingdom of heaven is about. Why? Because Jesus told us that the kingdom of heaven is like wheat and weeds growing *together* until the day has come for the weeds to be removed. Though the Master plants good seed, "while his men were sleeping, his enemy came and sowed weeds among the wheat and went away."[21] There is no doubt that the enemy of our souls comes and plants weeds among us. "The weeds are the sons of the evil one, and the enemy who sowed them is the devil."[22] Unfortunately, however, our tendency is to focus our attention on rooting out those weeds. But what did the Master tell His servants to do? They, in their misguided zeal, offered to rip them out then and there. Instead, the Master instructed them, "No, lest in gathering the weeds you root up the wheat along with them. Let both grow together until the harvest, and at harvest time I will tell the reapers, 'Gather the weeds first and bind them in bundles to be burned, but gather the wheat into my barn.'"[23] He not only told them not to do it, but He also explained *why* not to do it. Because if they did go ahead and pull the weeds out, they would risk damaging the wheat. And how many of us have stories of being among believers who were so obsessed about pulling out the weeds that we decided we didn't want anything to do with their God? So we must be careful to listen to the Master's warning.

Now some of you might be reading and thinking, "But what about: 'expel the wicked person from among you?'"[24] Absolutely! As children of God, we must watch our acquaintances and we must make sure that we do not become friends with the world. Truly, "friendship with the world is hostility toward God."[25] But the children of God do not keep themselves holy by constantly being critical of others or by being on a witch hunt for false doctrine. You don't keep your teenagers from seeking unhealthy relationships by teaching them to condemn others as "children of disobedience." You keep them safe from communing with people who would harm them by having them commune with you instead. You make them feel loved and appreciated so they don't have to go off trying to find that affirmation in other people. I don't imagine I would have done half of the things I did growing up if I had had a better relationship with my father.

It is tempting to want to advance the kingdom by tearing others down or by constantly being on the lookout for the lies. We don't want to be deceived so we remain hyper-vigilant against falsehood. That is a technique that I myself have tried so I can tell you from experience that it isn't a method that is very life giving. Instead, I have learned by the Word of God that there is a better way.

> But you, dear friends, by building yourselves up in your most holy faith and praying in the Holy Spirit, keep yourselves in God's love as you wait for the mercy of our Lord Jesus Christ to bring you to eternal life. Be merciful to those who doubt; save others by snatching them from the fire; to others show mercy, mixed with fear—hating even the clothing stained by corrupted flesh. To Him *who is able* to keep you from stumbling and to present you before His glorious presence without fault and with great joy—to the only God our Savior be glory, majesty, power and authority, through Jesus Christ our Lord, before all ages, now and forevermore! Amen. (Jude 20–25 NIV; emphasis mine)

BEING SECURE IN THE KINGDOM

As I've said before, all that is mine belongs to my children. They have not *earned* this right; it is by nature of being mine that they have access to all that I have to give. Yet for the time being, they are not in a position to receive all that is mine. They lack the understanding, the maturity, and even the ability to steward what it is I have to give them. This does not void the fact that I desire to give them all that I have. It does mean, however, that for a time, they will be limited in what they can receive. Again, this is not their *fault*. It is not a matter of being good or bad children. It is the nature of being young and needing to learn how to grow in their understanding of who I am and what it means to receive from me.

So I raise my children to know that they are loved and that their future is secure. Their father works diligently not only to provide for today but to also leave them an inheritance that they will enjoy tomorrow. The hope is that in convincing my children that they are provided for in love and in resources, they would grow up to be confident and mature adults. They would not be motivated by insecurities. They would not grow up hurting others out of fear or out of selfish ambition. They would grow to be secure in my love and know that they already have what they need so they are free to love and serve others. This desire is not a desire that I was raised into by my earthly father. It is the very desire of my Father in heaven.

This chapter can go on and on into a whole book about the wonders of the kingdom of heaven. In fact, there is already a whole book out there: the Bible. If after reading this you're still not sure what the kingdom of God is like and what a great gift it is, I *highly* recommend you crack open that Bible and take the time to really take in what God has to say about it. Ultimately, I want us to realize that this wonderful gift, like all of God's great gifts, is secure in Christ. I want *you* to be convinced that "when you believed in the Messiah, you were sealed with the promised Holy Spirit, who is *the guarantee of our inheritance* until God redeems His own possession for His praise and glory"[26] (emphasis mine). We need not fear. We need not be uncertain about our past, present, or future. We don't have to continue lashing out at others or live in constant worry that things won't work out for our good. Our Father in heaven has withheld no good thing from us. It is His good pleasure to give us His kingdom. From this moment forward, let us keep all this in our hearts. Let us live out our lives being kingdom minded. And this we will do by the power of His Holy Spirit, for His praise and glory. In Jesus's name, amen.

CHAPTER 8 REFLECTIONS

1. Has this chapter changed the way you understand the kingdom of heaven? How?

2. How does knowing that God has always wanted to gift us His kingdom change the way we view God throughout scripture?

3. Do you believe that the kingdom is in your midst? If so, how does this change your outlook on the life you're living now?

4. Do you feel secure in knowing that God the Father wants you to have an inheritance with Christ? Why or why not?

5. Are there still some insecurities you might have about your future? Why?

Prayer Invitation

It is a major understatement to say that God went through a lot of trouble to bring His kingdom to us. Having been separated from Him by sin and by hurt, He made a way through Jesus Christ. So now we live a new life as His children, comforted by His presence, secure in His reign over our lives as children of the kingdom of heaven. Let us pray that God would convince us of this reality. Where insecurity remains, let us pray that God would remove that by His promises. Pray that you would be given eyes that see beyond the current circumstances. Pray that God would increase your confidence in the certainty of His Heavenly kingdom and all that comes with it. In Jesus's name. Amen.

CHAPTER 9

GIVING HIS DISCIPLINE

*My child, don't reject the Lord's discipline, and don't be
upset when He corrects you. For the Lord corrects those He
loves, just as a father corrects a child in whom he delights.*
—Proverbs 3:11–12 (NLT)

Growing up, I was never really convinced that my dad loved me. Whenever I would do anything, he seemed to always have a harsh criticism about how I could have done better. He was very strict about standards, and he was very quick to discipline me whenever I failed to meet those standards. Now mind you, my dad never actually spanked me or anything. But he did have a way of being stern that made me wish that he spanked me instead. But it was difficult for my young heart to comprehend that my dad actually loved me very deeply because he was such a perfectionist. It seemed to me that he was so strict, and he was always more focused on disciplining me, rather than loving me. Eventually, however, once I had finally become an adult and was out experiencing life on my own, I realized that all of my dad's discipline was actually an expression of his love for me. In fact, for my dad, it was how he confirmed his love for me because it meant that he was taking an active role in molding me into a man of character.

Even after everything that was said and done during my

childhood, I tell my dad today that if I had to change one thing about growing up with him as my father, it would be that he didn't utter the words "I love you" enough. It wouldn't be that he was so strict or that he corrected me so often. It wouldn't be that he had such high standards for me as his only son. It was that he never helped me connect the dots by explicitly stating that the reason for his discipline was because he loved me and he wanted the best for me once I moved on to be a man.

Now that I have my own children, I understand. I see early on how they struggle with impulses to do wrong. My oldest son at one year old was always tempted to touch the things we explicitly told him not to touch. We would watch him as the urge consumed him until he either gave in or threw a miniature tantrum at the fact that he had to restrain himself. Now that the two of them are old enough to play together, my wife and I have to constantly intervene when one is struggling to share with the other. It seems the more they are aware and the more decisions they make on their own, the more I, as their loving father, have to step in and discipline them. And because I'm their father, I realize that I have never disciplined them with a desire to hurt them or upset them. As far as I can remember, I have always been motivated by a desire to help them live out and enjoy the life they were created for. The discipline I give my kids confirms that they are my children and I am their father. It confirms that I have a vested interested in their well-being and that I love them as my own.

Imagine then what it must mean when God our Father disciplines us. If my dad and I, two men corrupted by sin and our pasts, desire to keep our children from stumbling, wouldn't God our Father desire this even more? Of course! So He, like a loving father, disciplines His children. Never for their harm. Never to abuse them but to correct and refine their character and faith. I grew up not understanding this about my earthly father, and it was part of the reason that he and I had such a strained relationship. Could it be possible that sometimes our misunderstanding of our Heavenly Father's discipline strains our relationship with Him as well?

It is not too much of a stretch to imagine that our misconceptions about discipline can stand in the way of experiencing God's love through His loving correction. But we should not be discouraged by the Lord's discipline. In fact, we should be *encouraged* because it means that He really considers us His own. It means that He identifies us as His and desires that our lives would reflect that. At the end of the day, the Father's discipline is a beautiful expression of the Father's love.

FROM THE FATHER'S PERSPECTIVE

A big criticism that people have of God is that He is so wrathful in the Old Testament. Many people, even Christians, think there is a difference between God in the Old Testament and God in the New Testament. Because the Bible teaches that we now live under the covenant of grace, many of us misunderstand this to mean that God's grace only began when Jesus came to preach the gospel. So we picture God the Son as a timid and weak Rabbi who wouldn't hurt a fly and picture God the Father as an angry and violent God who is out to condemn all who disobey. But nothing could be farther from the truth, and I hope that by now you see this.

When we look at the story of God's love through the lens of the gospel, we see that God our Father is not against us; He is for us. We see that He never spared the rod because He has never desired our destruction. From the beginning of humankind's disobedience, God has always corrected and intervened. Instead of blind and violent wrath, we see the tale of God's children disobeying and God disciplining. Now "[f]or the moment all discipline seems painful rather than pleasant, but later it yields the peaceful fruit of righteousness to those who have been trained by it."[1] And we do see both parts of this scripture play out as true. Being cast out from the Garden, having a flood wipe out most of humanity, walking for decades in the wilderness, wars, and famine, etc. All these forms of discipline seem incredibly harsh. To the untrained child, it even seems unreasonable. However, when we take into account that all of human history was leading up to the point where God Himself would hang on the cross for us, we see that all that discipline yielded a "peaceful fruit of righteousness."

When we see God's discipline only from the perspective of a child, we understand that "it is a terrifying thing to fall into the hands of the living God!"[2] But when we chose to view His discipline from *His* perspective, we can know in our hearts that "as a man disciplines his son, so the Lord your God disciplines you."[3] Consider the whole story of God's love. What does it look like from His perspective?

We see that first He made everything perfectly for His children. He made humankind perfectly in His image, placing on him the glory of being a reflection of God Almighty. Then humankind disobeyed Him, and his disobedience cost him his life. He put humankind outside of His presence, but not without a promise to make right his wrong. Humankind witnessed for himself how by being distanced from his Father, he was able to fall deeper and deeper into rebellious sin and more and more into self-destructive behavior. So God cleansed him. He washed humankind clean and helped him start over. Then He gave humankind a promise. Humankind would be blessed and build many nations of kings who would know their Father. But it was necessary for God to lay down some ground rules. He gave humankind His Law. This Law would be humankind's caretaker. It would guide him as he grew and matured. He would break the rules time and again, and time and again, God would step in and discipline him.

God would follow him from the time of ignorant childhood to the point of adolescence where humankind was able to willingly choose his own path. Having learned and grown in the presence of his Father, humankind still chose to live a life apart from the wisdom of his Father. So God let him. He let him stray into bad company. He let His son do what he chose to do, and He let him experience the consequences. He let His child see that no one would love him as much as his Father loved him. And humankind seemed abandoned by His Father. "But when the fullness of time had come, God sent forth His Son, born of woman, born under the law, to redeem [humankind], so that we might receive adoption as sons."[4]

I can see in my own children that they don't fully understand why their father can get so mad sometimes. Why can't they do this? Why can't they do that? For the child who is constantly choosing to disobey, Dad can seem so mean! But as their father, I know why I do what I do. I have plans for them. Not to hurt them but to prosper them. Plans for a hope and future. I am willing to do "the hard right" of disciplining them to help them avoid the "easy wrong." I don't desire obedience so I can be puffed up; I want them to experience the joys of life so I place "a law" over them that will keep them in the path of peace. From *my* perspective as their father, their disobedience costs *them,* not me.

For the child, it is so easy to get filthy in their day-to-day activities. They eat messy, they play messy, and they're a mess by the time the day is done. But who is able to clean them? Their loving father. A child can run around all day saying and doing things without regard for consequence. But who is able to keep them safe and keep them from hurting themselves? Their loving father. The more the child can do, the more he wants to be free. I know that as a father, I *want* my child to experience that freedom. But not at the expense of his peace and joy. I know better than him that we have a way of misunderstanding freedom to mean we can do whatever we want. Like the Corinthians whom Paul had to rebuke, we think "everything is permissible!" to which the loving spiritual father replies, "but not everything is beneficial … not everything is edifying."[5] It makes a world of difference to see discipline from the Father's perspective. Rather than a God who is a meany, we see a God who disciplines those in whom He delights. We see a God who loves us as the Father loves His Son.

DO NOT SCORN THE LORD'S DISCIPLINE

It took me almost nineteen years to understand that my dad loved me. It wasn't just that I was finally nineteen years old but that by the time I was an adult, I had finally experienced enough of life to begin to understand what my dad was trying to instill in me when I was younger. Because he and I had such a rocky relationship, his discipline often seemed like he was adding insult to injury. It seemed that on top of the fact that he didn't spend intimate time with me, the only time he did spend he spent it correcting me. So I think it's understandable that I couldn't put two and two together and realize that he was actually trying to make the most of our time together by trying to make sure that he was building my character. I think that many times we as children of God fail to put the two together because we ourselves are not intimate with our Father.

We read so much about God's righteous anger in the Old Testament that we can make the mistake of thinking that God is just an angry God who spends His time smiting humanity. To make matters worse, we see Jesus as a soft and frail carpenter's Son who could never hurt a fly. So we distinguish Him from the "angry God" in the Old Testament and believe that somehow the God in the Old Testament is different from the God in the New Testament. The issue, however, is not that God changed toward us but that through Jesus we can now see more clearly the heart of God. We were once "alienated with a hostile attitude"[6] toward God, but now "we were reconciled to God by the death of His Son."[7] There was once a veil over the Old Covenant that kept us from being able to fully understand how it reflected the love of the Father. "But whenever a person turns to the Lord, the veil is removed,"[8] and we can now see that even in all the righteous anger, God is for us.

In fact, what we often lose sight of when we see God dealing with the people of the Old Covenant is that God's discipline against the Israelites was a fulfillment of His promise to His people. He promised them that He would be their God and they would be His chosen people. He would not only lead them into the Promised Land, but He would also discipline them for going astray. Every judgment we see, He promised to do so that His people who are called by His name would humble themselves and turn from their wicked ways so that He would hear from heaven, forgive their sins, and heal their land.[9] In keeping His promise of discipline, He was being faithful to His people and confirming them as His own. As the scripture explains, "If God doesn't discipline you as He does all of His children, it means that you are illegitimate and are not really His children at all."[10] It is *because* we are His that God is faithful to discipline us when we need it most.

Now we must not assume that all discipline is harsh. We should not make the mistake of thinking that every one of God's corrections is a severe spanking. The Lord "deal[s] gently with those who are ignorant and are going astray."[11] It wasn't always through famine or war that God corrected His people; it was more often with His Word. He would always put His Word on the lips of messengers who would warn His people that they were going astray, and they would be punished for it. God wasn't on a mission to hurt His people. He was on a mission to save them from sin and death. And to this day, He continues to use His Word as a way of disciplining us. That is why the Word says, "All Scripture is breathed out by God and profitable for teaching, for reproof, for correction, and for training in righteousness, that the man of God may be complete, equipped for every good work."[12]

I personally do not get joy out of spanking my children. As often as I can avoid spanking them, I do. But I will not "spare the rod" and allow my children to be destroyed. I see my Father's example, and I warn them first. I let them know that what they're doing is wrong. If they don't listen, I let them know that there will be a consequence for their continued disobedience. If they continue, I come near them so that they me see that I intend to discipline them if they do not relent. If they persist, I fulfill my commitment to them and provide the necessary correction. It is a gift of love that I would be faithful to keep my children on the right path.

In the end, my children know that I love them. We have a very strong relationship. Praise be to God! So when I discipline them, they still come back to hug me. They do not become insecure or afraid to come to me. They understand that I discipline them because I love them. I am not an angry dad who looks to take his anger out on his children. I am their loving father who is committed to helping them become all they were meant to become. Our Father in heaven is even more committed to us. He is faithful and just to forgive, and He is faithful and just to correct us. So let us come boldly before the throne of grace, increasing in our intimacy with our Father. Let us welcome His loving discipline and invite His confirmation over us as His legitimate children.

RESTING IN HIS DISCIPLINE

Ultimately, we need not be afraid of God's correction. It comes from the heart of the loving Father who desires that we would live in the joy and peace that come from obedience. God's correction does not loom over us like a belt waiting to come across our backsides. We are not under punishment but under reconciliation with God through Christ Jesus. He said to us, "Peace I leave with you, my peace I give unto you: not as the world giveth, give I unto you. Let not your heart be troubled, neither let it be afraid."[13] We rest in knowing that we have the peace that Christ earned through perfect obedience to the Father. We need not be afraid of judgment, because God the Son has stepped in on our behalf to be the One who obeys perfectly. Therefore, we can trust that what Jesus did was enough and remember that "[t]here is no fear in love, but perfect love casts out fear. For fear has to do with punishment, and whoever fears has not been perfected in love."[14]

We can be certain that our Heavenly Father will discipline us when necessary. When we in our stubbornness are led astray, He will correct us. But He does not do this for our harm. He does this so that we may be perfected in love. He is trying to teach us that we do not need to surrender our lives to sin, we do not need to dwell in our past life, and we can obey His life-giving Word and live under His constant peace and joy. God does not change. He has always corrected those who belong to Him. It may be a "dreadful thing to fall into the hands of the living God,"[15] but even more dreadful would it be to fall outside His loving embrace and to remain apart from Him. So let us not scorn the Lord's discipline. Instead, let us rest in His discipline and the peace that comes with knowing that His correction is His gift to us, confirming that we are His.

CHAPTER 9 REFLECTIONS

1. How does seeing discipline from the Father's perspective change your view on how He deals with us?

2. Do you still scorn the Lord's discipline? Why?

3. Are you comfortable in knowing that your Father's discipline is a confirmation of His love for you? Why or why not?

4. Are you living in fear of God's punishment? Why?

Prayer Invitation

I want to invite you to pray that the Lord would grant you rest in His discipline. Pray that God would confirm to you that His correction is not meant to destroy you or to provoke you but to help you see more of Him and to help you walk in the peace of obedience. Pray that God would shift your heart to no longer fear God's correction but to welcome it as part of the process of being perfected in His love. Pray that the Holy Spirit would remind you that no matter what, God's discipline is not a condemnation but a confirmation that you are a legitimate child of God. In Jesus's name. Amen.

CHAPTER 10

GIVING HIS ASSIGNMENT

Jesus answered, "The work of God is this:
to believe in the one He has sent."
—John 6:29 (NIV)

It is my hope, my intent, and my prayer that by now you understand what it means to be loved by the Father. I hope that you recognize any insecurities or wounds from your past that you may have been projecting onto your Father, and I hope you have cast them aside for the real heart of God. His heart says that while it is so very important that we recognize sin for what it is, it's so much more important that we recognize the power and desire that He has as our Father to forgive and to heal us from our sins. If at any point in time you become unsure of this, go back to His Word. It is His gift to you to help remind you of His deep eternal love that covers a multitude of sins. It is because of His deep love that He sent His Son to reveal Him to us. And more than that, He has sent His Holy Spirit to dwell with us and in us, to confirm to us the promise of being called children of God. And as His children, we are citizens of His kingdom. A kingdom that is advancing every day in our lives and in the world. And as it advances farther and farther, our Father continues to discipline us so that we may be prepared for every good work of the kingdom of heaven.

These good works are not meant to be a burden. They are not meant to replace everything we've talked about. In fact, the work of the Father cannot be fully understood until it is understood in the context of the gospel. Only in the reality of being forgiven through the blood of Jesus, born again by the power of the Holy Spirit, and brought into communion with God the Father can we then approach the so-called "Great Commission" with the peace and joy that God the Son showed us and promised to give us. We've been so conditioned to think of following Jesus in terms of being "good and faithful servants" that we forget that we follow Him into fellowship with the Father. But God willing, we will walk away from this discussion understanding what it means to be doing the works of the Father.

IDENTITY CRISIS

From the day they were conceived, my children have never had to work for what they have. They haven't paid the mortgage for the roof over their head, and they don't pay the bill at the store for the food that they eat or the clothes that they wear. They definitely don't pay for the toys in their toy box. Absolutely nothing they have did they work for. Of course not. They're only toddlers. Am I a fool to think that they won't ever have to work for a living? Not at all. But as long as they're in my house, I will provide everything they need, including the skills and wisdom they require so that one day they can go out and thrive as adults.

But what about the child of God? Does the child of God ever really outgrow His Father's house? Does the child of God ever mature to a point that he or she no longer needs his or her Father's provisions? No. God forbid. I may not always be there for my children to provide for them and care for them. I can't. I'm only human. But where my hand is too short, my Father's is more than sufficient to reach not only my children but all of His children . Because of this, the child of God does not work for a living; he or she works for love. Not to earn love but to celebrate it.

That being said, this idea of working to celebrate love is not incredibly common. Instead of asking questions like "How can you express your love for God through the work you do?" we ask questions like "What do you want to be when you grow up? What are you going to *do?*" Or even "What is your ministry?" We ask these questions even of our children, often before they're even old enough to understand what a career is. In our modern culture, and even among believers, productivity seems to be the gold standard for human value. Are you actually a productive member of society? If not, why would we keep you around? Are you working for the kingdom? If not, are you even really saved? We have career days when professionals come into the classroom to show off their respective fields in the hopes of captivating young minds early on and potentially recruiting them for future employment in the same field. We have tests to assess your "spiritual gifts" to see how we can increase your productivity. Because of this, people no longer consider work an expression of their love for God and for their fellow man; they think of work as the place where their identity is found.

This isn't really an issue exclusive to the West. In cultures throughout the world, what people do for their communities is often more important than who they are. It seems that as a whole, humankind is obsessed with the idea of work. More than that, it seems that people throughout the world find their identity in the work that they do. Even in cultures where the identity of children is associated with their father, the father's reputation is usually associated with the work he does. When people say that so and so is a "good man," they support their claim by mentioning the "good work" he does as their evidence.

It is no wonder that we have lost sight of God's original intent for work. It is no wonder that even among children of God people are often undergoing an identity crisis. We are growing up believing that our value is attached to the work we do. We mistakenly believe that our identity is found in our occupation for the kingdom. And this couldn't be farther from the truth! But in order to realize that, it has become necessary to review where our identity truly lies; we have to go back to why God made us in the first place.

BACK TO THE BEGINNING

I remember that I started doing my own chores around age six. At this age, I began washing my own clothes, cleaning my own bathroom, organizing my own bedroom, and sometimes cooking my own food. My mom says all the time that she was proud of her decision to teach me how to do these things because she didn't want me growing up unable to take care of myself. However, I remember six-year-old me being convinced that the only reason my mom had me was so that I could do chores around the house.

That may seem like a silly thought, and in fact, it *was* in my context, but it isn't far-fetched to imagine that someone would have children for the sole purpose of having extra hands to help around the house. This is actually very common in cultures around the world, especially more rural cultures where labor isn't easy to come by. More children mean more free labor, and it means more possibilities of being able to hand down the labor to future generations. It's not that these parents don't love their children. But one could see how these children would grow up thinking of their lives in terms of the work they were created to accomplish. They were born and raised to do work and to maintain what was built for them.

Some people have children in hopes that they could live vicariously through them. So much in their life they feel they didn't get to have, and they want to raise their children to have it instead. They attempt to instill in their children a desire for the things *they* desired growing up so that their kids could accomplish what they could not. They lay on their children a burden to perform in such a way that will lead to the parent finally being able to see their heart's desire come to fruition through their kids. The children grow up with the constant reminder that their parents are depending on them to succeed in order to have the success they couldn't.

Perhaps more tragically, some people didn't want the children they have. They had no plans to have them, and they may have even tried to do away with the child. They consider them a burden or an obstacle to the life they want to live. Out of some sense of moral or social obligation, they tolerate their little ones, counting down the days until they won't have to deal with them any longer. But whether by word or by deed, the child is aware that he is not wanted. He grows up wondering why. He grows up looking for acceptance in other people or in other things.

We've talked about this before, but so much of what we think about why God made us is shaped by how our parents raised us. If we were raised to think that our parents want us to work hard so we can carry on the family legacy, it will be easy for us to think that God made us for that reason. If we grew up having to fill our father's shoes so we could carry his dreams farther than he could, we will imagine that God is wanting us to do the same for Him. What's worse, if we grew up unwanted by our parents, treated like an accident, we may mistakenly assume that we were an accident to God. Considering the fact that our upbringing is so influential in our perception of who we are, these conclusions are not unreasonable. However, they remain inaccurate.

First of all, there is something *very* important that we can never forget. There is absolutely nothing that any of us could ever do *for* God that He *needs* us to do. As the apostle Paul explained to the Athenians, "The God who made the world and everything in it is the Lord of Heaven and earth ... And He is not served by human hands, as if He needed anything. Rather, He Himself gives everyone life and breath and everything else."[1] We are not here because our Father was short-staffed or because He couldn't carry anything out without us. We are here because He wants us to be.

He created everything before He created humankind. He was

able, with the sound of His voice, to bring everything into existence. This should put you at ease that He doesn't *need* you to help Him do His work. When it was all said and done and when He had blessed what He had made as good, *then* He created humankind. And He didn't just whip them up like it wasn't a big deal. He had a specific purpose. "Let us make humankind in our image, *to be like us.* Let them be masters over the fish in the ocean, the birds that fly, the livestock, everything that crawls on the earth, and over the earth itself!"[2] (emphasis mine). God made us to bear His image and glorify Him by ruling over all that He had *done* (past tense) so that His will would be done on earth as it is in heaven. Our identity was never meant to be the work we do. Our work was always meant to be a natural consequence of our identity as image bearers of God.

BEARING OUR FATHER'S IMAGE

When we look back at the first creation, we see the intent of God's heart for us to bear His image and walk into all the work that He had done. But by the time the Son of God came in the form of man, sin had so misconstrued the image of God in people's minds that they did not recognize Him when He stood before them. So it's fitting that the apostle John would begin his account of the gospel by taking us back to that first creation and reminding us that "through [Jesus] all things were made; without Him nothing was made that has been made. In Him was life, and that life was the light of all humankind."[3] Jesus was there when we were first made in God's image, and He came back to restore us to that reality.

As the founder and perfecter of our faith, Jesus not only paid for our sins and not only revealed the Father to us but also showed us what it looked like to be in perfect fellowship with Him and to reflect His image. "He is the reflection of God's glory and the exact likeness of His being."[4] When we look at the Son of God, we are looking at the perfect image of God the Father. The character, the actions, and the very nature of the Son are all a perfect reflection of the Father. Unhindered by sin and insecurity, Jesus Christ could not help but reveal the glory of the Father wherever He went. This was not a job that Jesus did; it was who He was. The eternal fellowship He enjoys with His Father is so perfect that whenever anyone meets Him, they meet the Father also!

But what about us? Lord knows that we can be less than godly! How could it be that we would be like Jesus, reflecting the image of God wherever we went? Because Jesus made it possible. The sin that once marred God's image on us He has cleansed with His blood. We are no longer the same people we were when we were corrupted by our sin nature, unable to display God's character because we were slaves to something that opposed Him in every way. We are set free by the Son of God, and now, "in this world we are like Jesus."[5] Though we once had a veil over our eyes that kept us from seeing God clearly, Jesus has removed the veil and given us eyes to see. And now, "all of us who have had that veil removed can see and reflect the glory of the Lord. And the Lord—who is the Spirit—makes us more and more like Him as we are changed into His glorious image."[6]

When we are born, we bear the image of our mother and father. But when we are born again, we bear the image of our Father in heaven. No longer do we reflect the sin nature that corrupts the flesh. We reflect the glory of the living God! We have "put on the new self, which is being renewed in knowledge after the image of its Creator."[7] The old creation has gone, and the new has come. And we did not do this of our own will. This is not something we earned. This is not something we worked hard at. This is what we were created for! What we weren't able to do on our own, God did "by sending His own Son in the likeness of sinful flesh to be a sin offering."[7] Jesus put Himself in our place and conformed Himself to *our* corrupted image (without letting Himself be corrupted), so that we could be conformed to *His* perfectly holy image.

So if we are confused about what it means to be made in the image of God, let us look to Jesus. He is able to show us clearly what it means. It means that we can "throw off everything that hinders and the sin that so easily entangles."[8] It means that we can bear the fruit of God: "love, joy, peace, patience, kindness, goodness, faithfulness, gentleness, self-control."[9] It means our minds are set on the things above not on the things below. Being made in the image of God is not something we do; it's something we are. And we *are* the light of the world. So let us let our light shine so that the world may see our good works and give glory to the Father.

HIS WORKMANSHIP

But what does all this have to do with God's assignment? What does this have to do with "the Great Commission"? Well, it has everything to do with it. If I were to ask you why you're here, what your purpose in life is, and what your "calling" is, what would you answer me? Would you tell me that your purpose is to glorify God? To spread the gospel? To make disciples of all nations? Let's say you answered yes to all of those questions. What would any of that really mean? What would it look like in your life?

For the child who is not deeply rooted in the love of the Father, it looks like someone who is caught up in trying to earn God's approval. They turn the good news into the news about all the things you have to *do* to get into heaven. They work diligently to labor for the kingdom in the hope that God would smile down on them and say, "Well done, my good and faithful servant." They are tired from working so hard. They criticize their brothers and sisters for not working hard enough. They walk around with a false sense of urgency. Without being rooted in love, they are like noisy cymbals clanging away about all that needs to be done, or else. Or else you won't be saved, or else you won't receive the blessing, or else you'll lose God's favor, or else you will be cast out.

When the work we do is not a natural expression of our identity in Jesus, who restored us to the image of God, our hearts cling to scripture about salt losing its flavor and being trampled underfoot or branches being broken off and cast into the fire. We miss the fact that the warnings about walking away from God or living in blatant disobedience are for those who are not being perfected in love. We remain unaware that so much of the loving rebuke found in the New Testament is sandwiched between phrases like "Grace and peace to you from God our Father and the Lord Jesus Christ"[10] and "the grace of the Lord Jesus be with you."[11] We don't experience life as children of God; we experience it as slaves or servants. And we struggle to accept what Jesus said when He said, "No longer do I call you servants, for the servant does not know what his master is doing; but I have called you friends, for all that I have heard from My Father I have made known to you."[12]

What then? Are we not supposed to labor for the kingdom? Of course we are! We are children of the Lord of the harvest, and we are told by Jesus to pray that *He* would provide laborers for the harvest. But it is essential that we understand that what we do for the kingdom is never a will of the flesh or the will of man but of God. "For we are *His* workmanship, created in Christ Jesus for good works, which God prepared *beforehand*, that we should walk in them"[13] (emphasis mine). In other words, God created us in His image so that we would walk into all the good works that *He* has already prepared. He didn't create us to find our identity in those works. He created us to walk in fellowship with Him *into* those works.

By this point, you should realize that the work you do is an inevitable consequence of your love for the Father. It is not something you convince yourself you have to do. It is something you do naturally as a child who is born of the Spirit. Again, Jesus told us very clearly, "Whoever abides in Me and I in him, he it is that bears much fruit, for apart from Me you can do nothing."[14] We shouldn't worry about bearing fruit for the kingdom if we are abiding in Jesus. We should be like the apostle Paul who wrote, "And I am sure of this, that He who began a good work in you will bring it to completion at the day of Jesus Christ."[15]

It is not you or me who do the work of God. It is God. As Jesus said, "My Father is always at His work to this very day, and I too am working."[16] For us, the work of God is to believe in the One He sent. And if we believe, we receive adoption as sons and daughters. And if we receive adoption, we receive the Holy Spirit of God. And if we receive Him, we receive power from God to fulfill His will on earth as it is in heaven. "And this is not your own doing; it is the gift of God, not a result of works, so that no one may boast."[17] But we're supposed to *prove* that we believe *by* our works, right? Wrong. *God* proves that we believe by the works *He* does through us.

Remember what Christ told us: Unless we are born again, we cannot see the kingdom. But if we are born again, we are born of the Spirit of God. And if we are born of the Spirit of God, He will abide in us and we will abide in Him. He is the Vine, and we are the branches. And if we remain in Him, we *will bear much fruit.* Either this is true or it isn't. Either we are convinced that we are children of God, born again in His image, being fruitful and multiplying, or we live in constant insecurity that we aren't doing enough to glorify God.

NOW WHAT?

Let's put everything we've discussed in this chapter and in this book in practical terms. As I've tried to express to you throughout, our faith in Jesus and our life as children of God is not just philosophy. It is not just religious theory. So I want to address that burning question of "Now what?"

When it comes to God's assignment over your life, always begin and end with the fact that you weren't created for a career path or for a job or even for a ministry. You were created to love God, to be loved by God, and to love others as you yourself are loved. Naturally, this means that He would invite you to steward what He has already done for you. This means that in all that you do in this life, you are *co-laboring* with Him. You don't have to live in constant fear that you're not doing enough. Be dedicated to a life of intimacy with the Father and you will come to understand the power of the Son's prayer, "not my will, but Yours, be done."¹⁸ We like to say in Christian circles that "you were made on purpose, for a purpose." And what we mean to say is that there is certainly a work that God intends to fulfill through each and every one of us. But that's the key to living in the peace of Jesus. That it is *God* who works to fulfill this work. Not you and not me.

Moving forward, if you have any questions about what God would have you do to glorify Him, "keep on asking, and you will receive what you ask for. Keep on seeking, and you will find. Keep on knocking, and the door will be opened to you."¹⁹ Be like David, who had set in his heart to build a temple for God, so he got started. Trust that your Father is able to send you a Nathan who can correct you if need be. Remember that you have not been given the spirit of the world but the Spirit of God. He is not a spirit of fear but of power and self-control. Trust these truths and step forward in faith. Your Father is able to keep you from stumbling. Don't get caught in *paralysis by analysis.* Walk forward as a child of God, being raised to reflect the image of God, who will be disciplined and perfected by God.

I know that some of you read this and still wonder if you preach enough, if you evangelize enough, if you read your Bible enough, if you pray enough, and if you're good enough. I hope by now you understand that it doesn't matter if *you* are enough. Jesus is enough. His grace is sufficient for you and me. What He came to do, to reveal the Father to us, to pay the price for our sins on the cross, to rise from the grave and confirm His power to give life, to show us the freedom and power in being a child of God, all of Him is enough. Some of us still suffer from insecurities that are brought about from our past. We worry that our sins have taken us too far away from the love of God and hope to make up for it in good works. I know some of you are worried that you might miss your calling. You're afraid that if you make the wrong choice, you're going to miss out on all that God has for you. You want to be a faithful son or daughter and don't want to be guilty of unbelief.

If that's still you, I want you to think back on all that we have talked about. I encourage you to go back to God's Word. Consider that while you were still an enemy of God, He gave His only Son for you. How much more will He give to you now that you are His child? If there is still pain from your past keeping you confused about the Father's heart, ask Him to heal you. If there are sins that keep you too ashamed to draw near to God, repent and ask Him to forgive you. Just don't let another day go by living in uncertainty, insecurity, and sin that keep you from the love of the Father.

In answering "Now what?" be convinced of your Father's heart. He is the One who made us in His image. He is the One who has revealed Himself to us to show us what that means. He has given so many good gifts, not the least of which is Himself, all so we would be confident in who we are to Him. It is in that confidence that we celebrate our love for Him by obeying His commandment "Therefore go and make disciples of all nations, baptizing them in the name of the Father and of the Son and of the Holy Spirit, and teaching them to obey everything I have commanded you. *And surely I am with you always, to the very end of the age*"[20] (emphasis mine).

CHAPTER 10 REFLECTIONS

1. Where does your identity lie? How does your identity determine your perception of work?

2. How can coming back to the gospel keep your identity rooted in Jesus? Why is that so important?

3. Why were you created? Were you created to live as a servant or as a child of God? What is the difference?

4. Having read this entire book, has your understanding of good works changed? How?

5. What can you do when you find yourself living outside of the confidence granted to you as an image bearer of God?

Prayer Invitation

Now that we've reached the end of our time together in this book, I want to invite you to pray a very important prayer:

> Our Father in heaven, may Your name be kept holy. May Your kingdom come soon. May Your will be done on earth, as it is in heaven. Give us today the food we need, and forgive us our sins as we have forgiven those who sin against us. And don't let us yield to temptation, but rescue us from the evil one.

HOW MUCH MORE?

As a father, my heart's desire is that my children would grow up confident in my love. I pray that I would be a man of such character that my children would be able to trust me and draw confidence from the fact that I am their father and they are my beloved children. The so-called burden is on me to show them who I am. To show them how much I would do for them, that I would give my life for them. The hope is that in doing so, they would have no need to doubt the love that their father has for them. They would not need to live with wounds from their father. They would not desire to sin against their father because sin would lose its appeal. They would grow up convinced of the healing power of forgiveness. They wouldn't grow up with an identity crisis. They would know who they are and whose they are and one day work from a place of love.

Now I know that this heart I have for my children, these good things I desire for them, they are not my own doing. It is the fruit of God's Spirit in me. It is my Father's heart. I am reminded every day when I look at my children that God is for me. I know that if my children asked me for bread, I would not give them a stone. Or if they asked me for a fish, I would not give them a snake. And I am reminded time and again that if I who was once evil, if I who was once insecure and in constant sin, if I know how to give my children good gifts when they ask, how much more will my

Father in heaven give me His loving forgiveness and healing, His Word, His Son, His Spirit, His kingdom, and His assignment? How much more will your Father in heaven give good things to those who ask Him?

ENDNOTES

Introduction
1   Matthew 7:11 (ESV)

Chapter 1 Wounds from Our Father
1   1 John 3:1 (ESV)
2   Matthew 11:28 (NIV)

Chapter 2 If You Then, Who Are Evil
1   Romans 6:23 (NIV)
2   2 Corinthians 5:21 (NIV)
3   James 1:14–15 (ESV)
4   Proverbs 6:27 (NLT)
5   John 8:34 (NASB)
6   Romans 7:21–24 (NIV)
7   1 John 3:4 (BSB)
8   Romans 3:11–12 (NIV)
9   Luke 18:19 (NASB)
10 1 John 1:8 (ESV)
11 Matthew 4:17 (ESV)
12 1 John 1:9 (ESV)

Chapter 3 Forgiveness and Healing
1   Matthew 11:4–5 (NIV)
2   Isaiah 53:5 (ESV)
3   Ephesians 1:5 (NLT)
4   2 Corinthians 5:21 (NLT)
5   1 Corinthians 6:11 (NLT)

6   John 3:18 (ESV)
7   Romans 8:1–2 (NIV)
8   1 Corinthians 6:19 (NIV)

Chapter 4 Born Again
1   John 3:3 (ISV)
2   John 3:6 (NLT)
3   Mark 10:24, 27 (NLT)
4   1 Peter 2:2 (ESV)
5   John 15:1–5 (CSB)
6   Matthew 28:19–20 (ESV)
7   John 13:3–5 (CSB)

Chapter 5 Giving His Word
1   Galatians 1:6–9 (GNT)
2   2 Peter 1:20–21 (ESV)
3   2 Timothy 3:16
4   Romans 15:4 (ESV)
5   John 5:39 (NIV)
6   John 10:35 (NASB)
7   Psalm 119:14–16 (NIV)
8   John 17:17 (GNT)
9   Hebrews 4:12 (NIV)
10   Matthew 4:4 (NET)
11   Ephesians 3:18 (NIV)
12   Hebrews 5:13 (NIV)
13   Hebrews 6:1–3 (NIV)
14   Psalm 34:8 (KJV)
15   Psalm 119:105 (NKJV)

Chapter 6 Giving His Son
1   John 14:6–7 (BSB)
2   John 1:18 (NLT)
3   John 14:9 (NLT)
4   John 5:19 (NLT)
5   Hebrews 4:15 (CEV)
6   Matthew 16:15 (NIV)
7   Revelation 1:8 (CSV)

8   Mark 14:62 (NLT)
9   Matthew 11:27 (GNT)
10 John 1:18 (NLT)
11 Matthew 4:17 (ESV)
12 John 8:11 (NKJV)
13 2 Corinthians 5:21 (NLT)
14 2 Corinthians 1:20 (NLT)
15 1 John 4:10 (NIV)
16 2 Corinthians 3:18 (NIV)

Chapter 7 Giving His Spirit

1   Ezekiel 36:27 (NIV)
2   Romans 8:16 (NKJV)
3   2 Corinthians 1:22 (NLT)
4   Luke 11:20 (CSB)
5   Romans 5:10 (NIV)
6   John 3:31 (NIV)
7   1 Corinthians 2:10 (NET)
8   Romans 8:5 (ISV)
9   2 Peter 1:21 (ESV)
10 1 John 3:19–20, 24 (NIV)
11 John 3:6 (NKJV)
12 2 Corinthians 5:17 (NIV)
13 John 8:36 (NLT)
14 John 15:3 (ESV)
15 1 Corinthians 6:11 (ESV)
16 2 Corinthians 13:14 (NIV)

Chapter 8 Giving His Kingdom

1   Matthew 4:17 (ESV)
2   Revelation 4:8 (NIV)
3   John 18:36 (ESV)
4   Genesis 17:6–7 (NIV)
5   Exodus 19:6 (NIV)
6   1 Peter 2:9 (NIV)
7   Mark 4:30 (NIV)
8   Matthew 13:45–46 (ESV)
9   Matthew 6:32–33 (NLT)

10   Romans 8:32 (NASB)
11   Luke 15:31 (BLB)
12   James 4:2–3 (NLT)
13   Romans 5:3–5 (ESV)
14   Matthew 6:9–11 (KJV)
15   Luke 17:20–21 (NIV)
16   Luke 11:20 (HCSB)
17   Romans 12:2 (ESV)
18   Ephesians 3:14, 16–19 (ESV)
19   Matthew 16:18 (ESV)
20   Philippians 1:6 (NIV)
21   Matthew 13:25 (ESV)
22   Matthew 13:28–29 (ESV)
23   Matthew 13:29–30 (ESV)
24   1 Corinthians 5:13 (NIV)
25   James 4:4 (BSB)
26   Ephesians 1:13–14 (ISV)

Chapter 9 Giving His Discipline

1   Hebrews 12:11 (ESV)
2   Hebrews 10:31 (HCSB)
3   Deuteronomy 8:5 (BSB)
4   Galatians 4:4–5 (ESV)
5   1 Corinthians 10:23 (BSB)
6   Colossians 1:21 (ISV)
7   Romans 5:10 (ESV)
8   2 Corinthians 3:16 (CSB)
9   2 Chronicles 7:14
10   Hebrews 12:8 (NLT)
11   Hebrews 5:2 (HCSB)
12   2 Timothy 3:16–17 (ESV)
13   John 14:27 (KJV)
14   1 John 4:18 (ESV)
15   Hebrews 10:31 (NIV)

Chapter 10 Giving His Assignment

1   Acts 17:24, 25 (NIV)
2   Genesis 1:26 (ISV)

3   John 1:3-4 (NIV)
4   Hebrews 1:3 (ISV)
5   1 John 4:17 (NIV)
6   2 Corinthians 3:18 (NLT)
7   Colossians 3:10 (ESV)
8   Hebrews 12:1 (NIV)
9   Galatians 5:22-23 (ESV)
10 Romans 1:7; 1 Corinthians 1:3; 2 Corinthians 1:2; Ephesians 1:2; Philippians 1:2; Colossians 1:2; 1 Thessalonians 1:1; 2 Thessalonians 1:2; Philemon 3; Revelation 1:4, 5 (various respective versions)
11 1 Corinthians 16:23; 2 Corinthians 13:14 (various respective versions)
12 John 15:15 (ESV)
13 Ephesians 2:10 (NAS 1977)
14 John 15:5 (ESV)
15 Philippians 1:6 (ESV)
16 John 5:17 (NIV)
17 Ephesians 2:8-9 (ESV)
18 Luke 22:42 (ESV)
19 Luke 11:9 (NLT)
20 Matthew 28:20 (NIV)

Printed in the United States
by Baker & Taylor Publisher Services